THE ROMANTIC
PRAIRIE COOKBOOK

THE ROMANTIC
PRAIRIE COOKBOOK

Field-fresh recipes and homespun settings

FIFI O'NEILL

PHOTOGRAPHY BY MARK LOHMAN

CICO BOOKS
LONDON NEW YORK

To my sons, Ron and Matt,
with all my forever love.

xoxo Mom

If you can talk with crowds and keep your virtue,
  Or walk with Kings—nor lose the common touch,
If neither foes nor loving friends can hurt you,
  If all men count with you, but none too much;
If you can fill the unforgiving minute
  With sixty seconds' worth of distance run,
Yours is the Earth and everything that's in it,
  And—what is more—you'll be a Man, my son!

Rudyard Kipling, **IF**

Published in 2012 by CICO Books
An imprint of Ryland Peters & Small Ltd

20–21 Jockey's Fields   519 Broadway, 5th Floor
London WC1R 4BW   New York, NY 10012

www.cicobooks.com

10 9 8 7 6 5 4 3 2 1

Text © Fifi O'Neill 2012
Design and photography © CICO Books 2012

A CIP catalog record for this book is available from the
Library of Congress and the British Library.

ISBN 978 1 908170 17 0

Printed in China

Editor: Gillian Haslam
Copy editor: Lee Faber
Designer: Christine Wood
Photographer: Mark Lohman

CONTENTS

Introduction

Only after the last tree has been cut down; Only after the last fish has been caught; Only after the last river has been poisoned; Only then will you realize that money cannot be eaten.

Cree Indian prophecy

With knowledge comes understanding. Though this is true of anything, it's crucial when it comes to the food we eat. The case for local food and the need to protect both humans and wildlife from the hazards from pesticides and biologically engineered produce has been made over and over. The benefits of no travel (a typical carrot has to travel 1,838 miles to reach most dinner tables), no artificial preservatives, and no genetically modified organisms are measurable.

The Romantic Prairie Cookbook champions environmental harmony and celebrates the stewardship of the land by using homegrown, flavorful ingredients taken directly from field to table, as it was customary centuries ago when living off the land and home cooking were essential to survival. This time-honored tradition brings to the forefront the unique talents of a collection of artisanal practices—from gardening to harvesting, baking, cheese making, preserving, pickling, and more. Recipes, steeped in the modest but imaginative and hearty heritage of the prairie, showcase the home cooks' and artisans' passion and respect for creating healthy, tasty, and satisfying dishes.

Today, even city dwellers who don't have a garden strive to grow herbs and vegetables in pots on a window sill, on a balcony or a roof-top terrace, or by joining a community garden. And the ever-growing numbers of local farmers' markets also afford them the opportunity to cook with fresh-from-the-fields fruits and vegetables and enjoy artisanal products like cheese and breads. On weekends, pick-your-own farms and roadside stands offer another opportunity to shop for local goods. Cold-storage crops, such as apples, cabbages, winter squash, and potatoes, allow for winter freshness, while fruit preserves and pickled vegetables keep summer's goodness on hand.

Food fads come and go. The only "trends" the home cooks featured in this book follow are those rooted in family traditions and the respect for the land and its inhabitants, may they be humans or animals. They also share a collaborative effort for sustainable local production and consumption, a common devotion to good simple food, and the belief that there is something unique about harvesting homegrown crops that connects them to the earth and their place. Through their thoughtful recipe choices, they create seasonal dishes that romance regional ingredients, satisfy our needs for flavors, and comfort body and soul.

But there is yet another fundamental element to this genuine and generous way of cookery. One that creates and maintains a link to childhood and the lessons learned growing up on harvests from grandma's garden, stirring a pot under mom's watchful eye, or gathering still-warm eggs from an aunt's chicken coop. There is a determination to reclaim such simple yet powerful experiences for their own children, to turn back the clock to a simple and healthier time, to reject the machine of the supermarket in a grass roots' effort to restore a safe environment and know where their food comes from.

Just as the French writer Marcel Proust wrote about the emotional connection between food (in his case a madeleine, a dainty little cookie) and remembrance, a fragrant herb, an aromatic stew slowly simmering, or the taste of a favorite cake can unleash images of these dedicated cooks' childhoods and contribute to the legacy they are creating for their children and for the well-being of the earth.

And suddenly the memory returns. The taste was that of the little crumb of madeleine, which on Sunday mornings, when I went to say good day to her in her bedroom, my aunt Léonie used to give me, dipping it first in her own cup of lime-flower tea…And as soon as I had recognized the taste of the piece of madeleine, immediately the old grey house upon the street, where her room was, rose up like a stage set…and with the house the town…the streets along which I used to run errands, the country roads we took when it was fine… sprang into being, town and gardens alike, from my cup of tea.

Marcel Proust, *Remembrance of Things Past*

Proust's perception relates so well to the meaning of this book because it illustrates the value and timelessness of the precious examples set by family traditions.

It is my hope that *The Romantic Prairie Cookbook* will offer a little insight into creating your own and your children's memorable "madeleine moments," in savoring yesterday and today, and will inspire you to sow the seeds, both real and virtual, of tomorrow.

Take only what you need and leave the land as you found it.

Arapaho saying

He who distinguishes the true savor of his food can never be a glutton;
he who does not cannot be otherwise.

Henry David Thoreau

chapter 1
starters and snacks

Grilled Chicken Pasta Salad

The fact that Rebecca Ersfeld and Donna Jenkins live in different states doesn't lessen the two friends' long-time ritual of cooking together. When the warmer weather arrives, Donna, who lives in Indiana, often packs up baskets of vegetables from her farm and makes weekend trips to Rebecca's Illinois home where the pair gather herbs from Rebecca's herb garden, and cook up favorite dishes from flavor-packed homegrown ingredients.

1 Heat a grill to high heat. If cooking indoors, use a cast iron skillet (frying pan).

2 Bring a large pan of water to a boil, add a pinch of salt and the pasta, and cook until al dente, about 9–11 minutes.

3 In a small mixing bowl, mix the garlic, steak seasoning, Tabasco, Worcestershire sauce, and 2 tbsp of the vinegar. Whisk in ¼ cup/60ml of the olive oil. Divide the mixture into 2 bowls. Add the sliced onions to one, and the chicken cutlets to the other. Toss to coat and marinate for a few minutes.

4 In a salad bowl, combine the mustard and the remaining 3 tbsp of vinegar with a little salt and pepper. Whisk in the remaining ¼ cup/60ml olive oil, and then add the Parmesan.

SERVES 8–10

8 oz/225g bowtie pasta (farfalle)
3 garlic cloves, peeled and chopped
2 tbsp steak seasoning
2 tsp Tabasco sauce (more if you prefer spicier food)
3 tbsp Worcestershire sauce
⅓ cup/75ml red wine vinegar
½ cup/120ml extra-virgin olive oil
2 large yellow onions, cut into thick slices
6 thinly-cut chicken breast cutlets (paillards)
2 tbsp Dijon mustard
ground black pepper
¼ cup/25g Parmesan, grated
1 tbsp extra-virgin olive oil
2 bunches of arugula (rocket)
1 small head radicchio
2 cups/25g fresh basil
¼ cup/15g fresh flat-leaf parsley
3 celery sticks
1 pint/300g grape (baby plum) tomatoes
8 oz/225g Mozzarella cheese, grated
sea salt
crusty baguette chunks, to serve
1 cup/115g pine nuts, to serve, optional

5 Once the pasta is cooked, drain it thoroughly and add it to the salad bowl with the dressing, and toss to coat.

6 In a skillet (frying pan), heat the 1 tbsp olive oil, add the onion slices, and cook until they are soft and well-caramelized.

7 Grill the chicken until done (about 3–4 minutes on each side). Remove both the onions and the chicken to a cutting board, and allow them to rest for about 5 minutes. Coarsely chop the onions and grilled chicken, and add them to the pasta.

8 Add the arugula, radicchio, basil, parsley, celery, and grape tomatoes. Toss to coat with the dressing. Add the Mozzarella cheese and a little more salt and pepper.

9 Serve with chunks of crusty baguette.

Variation

For a fun flavor twist, add 1 cup/115g pine nuts to the finished salad.

Rustic Turkey Sandwich with Broccoli-Peanut Salad

Sarah and Darius Anderson and their little boy Tyge live in one of the first five houses built in Sonoma, California. Their 1875 farmhouse reflects their mutual love of home and earth—Sarah owns Chateau Sonoma, a country French antique shop, and Darius thrives in creating beautiful spaces. Sarah describes her home as cozy and welcoming "like a bear hug when you walk in the door." The couple also has a passion for homegrown produce and the environment.

1 Make the salad (this needs to be left overnight). Put the broccoli in a colander and wash under cold running water.

2 Put a small amount of fresh water in a medium saucepan and add the broccoli. Bring to a boil and blanch for 3 minutes. Drain and put the broccoli in a bowl of ice water to stop the cooking process and retain its bright green color. Drain and transfer to a salad bowl.

3 In a small bowl, combine the olive oil, vinegar, Tabasco, sugar, and onion. Mix well and season with salt and pepper. Add dressing to the cooled broccoli and toss to coat.

4 Wrap the salad bowl with plastic wrap (clingfilm) and marinate overnight in the refrigerator.

5 Make the sandwich. In a bowl, mix the mustard, mayonnaise, rosemary, and paprika until smooth and well combined.

6 Spread half the mixture over one of the bread slices. Add the turkey and arugula. Spread the rest of the mixture on the other slice, flip over, and cover the filling.

7 Serve immediately, or wrap tightly in plastic wrap (clingfilm) and keep refrigerated until ready to serve.

8 Sprinkle the salad with the peanuts just before serving.

For the salad:

SERVES 6

2 lb/900g broccoli (mostly florets with just a bit of peeled stems)
½ cup/120ml extra-virgin olive oil
¼ cup/60ml apple cider vinegar
¼ tsp Tabasco sauce
1 tsp sugar
1 tbsp diced onion
sea salt and ground black pepper
½–¾ cup/50–75g honey roasted peanuts, to serve

For the sandwich:

MAKES 1

½ tbsp whole grain mustard
½ tbsp mayonnaise
¼ tsp finely chopped fresh or dried rosemary
¼ tsp paprika
2 thick slices rustic bread, or bread of choice
4 oz/115g thinly sliced cooked turkey
5 sprigs arugula (rocket)

Wilted Lettuce with Hot Bacon Dressing

Lovingly worn and gently splattered, family cookbooks hold much more than priceless handwritten recipes. They bring back a way of life when making do and inventiveness were often the main ingredients. These homespun traditions are not lost on Joy Waltmire, who puts them to practice in her own Illinois farmhouse and passed them on to her daughter, Angela Reed, an avid gardener and skilled cook herself. Joy's grandma's Bauer's Wilted Lettuce salad is one of the many recipes that brings back sweet childhood memories.

1 Brown the bacon in a pan over medium heat. Remove from the pan and reserve the drippings.

2 In a bowl, combine the lettuce, onion, bacon, cranberries, and pecans.

3 In a pan set over medium heat, add the vinegar, water, and bacon drippings and heat to boiling. Add the sugar and stir until dissolved.

4 Pour the hot dressing over the lettuce mixture and serve immediately.

SERVES 4

For the salad:
8 oz/225g bacon (streaky bacon)
4 cups/115g shredded garden lettuce
1 small onion, peeled and finely chopped
½ cup/50g dried cranberries
½ cup/50g chopped pecans

For the dressing:
¼ cup/60ml vinegar
½ cup/120ml water
4 tbsp sugar

Tomato Mozzarella Salad

The Kirkpatricks' California home and its setting are right out of the Italian countryside. Not a complete surprise considering that when Elizabeth married her Italian-born husband, Giampiero, the couple lived in a farmhouse in the Tuscan hills for several years before returning to the San Francisco Bay area in 1994. "I was longing for Italy and wanted to be in an old stone house surrounded by vineyards and gardens," Elizabeth says. But the similarities with Giampiero's native land don't end with the house design or the grounds abounding with flowers and vegetables. Giampiero also brought his love of fresh food together with recipes passed on from one generation to the next. Served al fresco in the sunny garden or family-style indoors, his culinary delights embody both California's distinctive freshness and Italy's characteristic flavors.

Arrange overlapping slices of tomatoes and mozzarella on a large platter. Sprinkle with salt, pepper, and basil and drizzle with the olive oil.

SERVES 6

3 large ripe tomatoes, peeled and sliced ¼ inch/5mm thick

10 oz/280g fresh mozzarella, sliced ¼ inch/5mm thick

4 tbsp finely chopped fresh basil leaves

¼ cup/60ml extra-virgin olive oil

sea salt and ground black pepper

Mixed Salad Greens with Poppy Seed Dressing

Tracey Leber credits her father for her love of gardening and her grandmother for her cooking skills. "My grandfather was an avid gardener and passed on his knowledge and passion to my dad, who in turn, passed it on to me. As soon as our long-awaited Illinois spring arrives, I am out digging in the dirt and continue to steal moments to linger in the garden until the last day of autumn. I only garden organically and completely support the idea that growing your own produce helps to create a better environment," she says.

Just like her grandma Ann Desideri, Tracey cooks everything from scratch. "What began as a means of controlling exactly what ingredients did (and didn't) go into a recipe, became a way for me to actually make more nutritious choices for my family as well. When you cook from scratch you know exactly what goes into your family's food! Not only everything tastes better but it's better for us as well."

1 Wash the salad leaves and spin dry. Combine all salad ingredients in a large bowl.

2 Mix all the dressing ingredients in a jar with a tight lid. Shake vigorously to blend.

3 Put the olive oil in a skillet (frying pan) set over medium heat. Add the slivered almonds and cook until golden brown, making sure they don't burn. Set aside.

4 Just before serving, toss with the poppy seed dressing.

SERVES 4

2–3 cups mixed salad leaves

11-oz/300g can mandarin oranges, drained or same quantity fresh mandarin oranges

6–8 strips (rashers) bacon, cooked until crisp and crumbled

4 tbsp slivered (flaked) almonds, toasted in 1 tsp extra-virgin olive oil

For the poppy seed dressing:

½ cup/120ml extra-virgin olive oil

6 tbsp/90ml apple cider vinegar

¾ cup/170g granulated sugar

1 small onion, diced

½ tsp Dijon mustard

¼ tsp sea salt

1 tbsp poppy seeds

Radish and Amaranth Salad

Lulu Tapp is passionate about fresh ingredients, especially when it comes to herbs and any vegetables she can grow in her small courtyard. She makes up for the space limitations by cultivating her favorites in pots, buckets, and even an old bathtub. Fortunately, the balmy southern California weather allows for a long growing season, and, when her production dwindles, Lulu goes to a nearby farmers' market to supplement her own crops. Just-snipped chives and tiny tomatoes plucked minutes before serving bring their distinctive goodness to her simple radish salad. Silky amaranth adds a note of vivid color and a pleasing sweetness.

1 This salad is a layered dish. First, arrange the radishes as desired, then the tomatoes, then the chives.

2 Drizzle with the olive oil and lemon juice and season with salt and pepper.

3 Gently lay down the amaranth. It's essential to add the olive oil, lemon juice, salt and pepper and the amaranth last. If not, you will weigh down the amaranth, and it will lose its airy, pretty texture.

SERVES 2

5 French breakfast radishes, quartered lengthwise

5 ordinary red radishes, thinly sliced

5 cherry tomatoes, halved

2 tsp snipped fresh chives

2 tbsp extra-virgin olive oil (or to taste)

juice of ½ lemon

sea salt and ground black pepper

organic red amaranth sprouts (if amaranth is not available, other organic sprouts can be substituted)

Summer Squash Ribbons with Squash Blossom Pesto

SERVES 4 AS A STARTER

3 x 6-inch/15cm yellow squash (courgettes), Gold Bar or Zephyr, if available, cut lengthwise in ⅛-inch/3mm thick ribbons

For the pesto:

14 large squash blossoms
½ cup/50g toasted slivered (flaked) almonds
⅔ cup/50g freshly grated Parmesan
juice and zest of 1 lemon
4 tbsp extra-virgin olive oil
sea salt and ground black pepper

For the dressing:

1 tsp Dijon mustard
¼ cup/60ml Champagne vinegar
1 small shallot, chopped
⅔ cup/150ml extra-virgin olive oil
sea salt

Sarah and Darius Anderson believe that food is a demonstration of love, and that simple pleasures are often the most satisfying. For Sarah, one of nine children raised on a farm, growing food was an essential part of the family's lifestyle; a tradition she followed with the creation of her lush and plentiful Sonoma garden. Row after row of vegetables are tended with great care, and supply more crops than one family could ever consume, which led Sarah and Darius to share their bounty with many through a weekly farmers' market and their cooking school, Ramekins.

1 First make the pesto. Take 10 squash blossoms and place them in a food processor along with half of the almonds. Pulse five or six times, scraping down the sides of the bowl until chopped finely.

2 Add the grated Parmesan, the lemon zest, and 2 pinches of salt; pulse two more times. Slowly add the olive oil a little at a time until the pesto resembles a thick sauce.

3 Spoon into a small bowl and reserve for later. This can be made up to one day in advance. Add a splash of lemon juice just before serving.

4 Make the dressing. Put the Dijon mustard and the Champagne vinegar into a bowl. Whisk together so the mustard is dissolved, then add the shallot and let stand for 10 minutes. Slowly whisk in the olive oil, and season with a pinch of salt.

5 Prepare the squash. Heat an outdoor grill or grill pan set over 2 burners on the stove. Oil the grill by brushing it with a lightly oiled paper towel.

6 Carefully place the squash on the grill, a couple at a time, and grill each side for about 30 seconds to 1 minute, or until the squash looks soft, but not mushy. Remove from the grill and place on a baking sheet lined with parchment, and sprinkle with salt. Repeat until all the squash is grilled.

7 To assemble, spoon the pesto onto a large serving platter. Fold the squash ribbons individually into little bundles on the baking sheet and spoon a small amount of dressing over each one.

8 Once all have been dressed, place them on the platter over and around the pesto. Garnish with the 4 remaining squash blossoms torn into small pieces, and sprinkle with the reserved toasted almonds.

Prosciutto with Fresh Figs

For Giampiero and Elizabeth Kirkpatrick, fresh figs and prosciutto is but one of the many summer dishes inspired by Giampiero's Italian family's traditions. Though he does not cure his own prosciutto—"just buy the very best," he advises —the figs are grown on the couple's property.

SERVES 6

6 fresh ripe figs, halved
6 paper-thin slices of high-quality prosciutto (about 1 oz/25g each)

Arrange the figs and prosciutto on a serving platter. Serve at room temperature.

Summer Succotash

This quick, colorful dish brings summer to the table. Lulu Tapp keeps fresh-frozen lima beans on hand for convenience, but always uses fresh tomatoes and herbs. Served hot as a side, or cold as a salad, this versatile mix embodies the simplicity and flavors of the season.

1 Pour the olive oil in a nonstick pan, add the bell peppers and sweat for 3 minutes.

2 Add the corn kernels and sweat for 3 minutes.

3 Add the cherry tomatoes and sweat for 3 minutes.

4 Add all the remaining ingredients except the bacon and cook together for an additional 3 minutes, then add the bacon, if using. Serve hot or cold.

SERVES 4

1½ tbsp extra-virgin olive oil

2 red or yellow bell peppers, cored, seeded, and diced

kernels from 2 ears of corn (sweetcorn)

6 cherry tomatoes, halved

1 cup/225g canned or frozen lima beans (butter beans)

2–3 scallions (spring onions), white parts only, chopped

1 large clove garlic, chopped

1 tbsp sherry vinegar

¼ cup/5g chopped fresh basil

a pinch of cayenne pepper

4 slices bacon, diced and cooked until crisp (optional)

sea salt and ground black pepper

Pumpkin Soup with Cilantro Oil

Twenty yeas ago, Barbara Jacksier, her husband Everett Chasen, their son Fred, and her mother Ruth, left Brooklyn, New York, for Clifton, Virginia. Barbara had lived in the city her entire life, but when her husband was offered a job in Washington, DC, she welcomed the opportunity to give the country life a chance. They purchased a home on five acres of land and, as the saying goes, the rest is history. Barbara quickly fell under the spell of the simpler, nature-grounded lifestyle and its many benefits. In no time she designed and planted a large vegetable garden. Among her most productive crops were culinary herbs, salad fixings, peas, beans, chard, kale, and edible flowers. A few years after the move, Fred's class raised baby chicks. Instead of sending their chicks to a local farm, Fred and a few of his friends brought them to Barbara. An old playhouse was converted to a chicken coop, and fresh eggs were added to the family's pantry.

Fall is a special time at "Foxwood Farm." Guests are invited to sample Barbara's harvest, and discover how good homegrown herbs and vegetables taste. It all culminates with a special Thanksgiving dinner where Barbara, Fred, Everett, and Ruth welcome some very fortunate friends who gladly give thanks for the family's flavor-packed homegrown offerings and wholeheartedly toast the city girl turned country girl.

1 In a large stockpot, melt the butter over medium heat. Add the onion and cook until soft, 5–10 minutes. Reduce heat, then add the pumpkin purée, water, coconut milk, and salt. Mix well. Let simmer for 30 minutes. Season with curry powder, ginger, and rosemary. Mix well and simmer for another 10 minutes. Add salt and pepper to taste, if desired.

2 Place the cilantro and oil in a food processor fitted with a steel blade and process until liquefied. Pour into a small bowl. Place the green pepper in a food processor fitted with a steel blade and process until puréed. Add the pepper purée to the cilantro oil to taste and pour into a serving cruet.

3 Ladle the soup into warmed bowls and drizzle a little cilantro oil on top of each serving.

SERVES 6–8

For the soup:

4 tbsp/55g butter

1 small onion, finely chopped

2 cups/450g pumpkin purée (fresh or canned)

1 quart/1 liter water

2 x 14-oz cans/800ml coconut milk

½ tsp salt

1 tsp curry powder

½ tsp ground ginger

1 teaspoon dried rosemary, pulverized in a spice grinder

sea salt and finely ground white pepper (optional)

For the herb oil:

1 cup/15g fresh cilantro (coriander) or basil leaves

4 tbsp olive oil

1 fresh mild Italian sweet or cubanelle hot green pepper, cooked until tender

Tip

The soup can be made ahead of time and reheated over low heat or in a microwave.

Roasted Butternut Squash Soup

Erin and Jason Shepherd, their 5-year old son Jacob, and dog, Belle, live blissfully among the chickens and pigs they raise on their idyllic North Carolina homestead, aptly named "Harmony Farm." Though Jason grew up helping his mom in the kitchen, the former firefighter's interest in food turned into a passion while recuperating from an accident that ended his career. "For six months I watched various TV cooking programs," he explains. "One chef, Emeril Lagasse, had a show 'Emeril Live,' which was where I learned the basics of cooking. I taught myself all of the sauces and the principles of all soups. I recall the first recipe I created: I didn't particularly enjoy my mom's chili because it was too sweet, so I came up with my own. I can remember my dad enjoying my chili more than my mom's."

To this day Jason does most of the cooking in the Shepherd household. "He is a more adventurous and creative cook than I am," Erin says. "However, I love to bake. We often cook meals together for our family members as their birthday present. Who doesn't appreciate a good, home-cooked meal? It's better than a store-bought gift."

Living the simple lifestyle equates with self-sufficiency, but also provides the kind of upbringing Jason and Erin favor for their son. "We are able to raise Jacob in an environment where he learns to respect the land and the animals that inhabit it. In order to receive from nature, we must all give back. The sanctuary we provide to bluebirds, woodpeckers, and wood ducks is our way of giving back," Jason says.

Deceptively easy to make and always a big success with guests (and one of Erin's favorites), this soup shows up Jason's skills at building up the flavors in his dishes. An immersion blender makes it very easy to transform the cooked ingredients into a soup right in the pot. And this soup freezes well, so any leftovers can be saved for another time, though it's so delicious, you'll want to eat it all up.

1 Preheat the oven to 350°F/180°C/gas mark 4.

2 Cut the squash in half lengthwise and scoop out the seeds. Drizzle 2 tbsp oil on the flesh of the squash, then season liberally with 1 tsp each of salt and pepper.

3 Place the squash flesh-side down on a baking sheet and roast for 1 hour 15 minutes. Remove from oven and let cool.

4 Meanwhile, heat remaining 1 tbsp oil in a Dutch oven or large stockpot over medium heat. Sauté the carrot, onion, and cumin for about 10 minutes, or until onion is translucent. Season with remaining salt and pepper.

5 Scoop the roasted squash from skin and add to the sautéed vegetable mixture. Add the chicken stock. With an immersion blender, purée the mixture to the desired consistency. Alternatively, if no immersion blender is available, the contents of the pot can be transferred in small batches into a blender and puréed. Keep warm.

6 Make the fried carrots. In a small pan, heat the peanut oil to 350°F/180°C. Drop the carrot shavings into the hot oil, frying for 2–3 minutes.

8 Remove the carrots from the pan with a slotted spoon and drain on paper towels (kitchen paper), pressing gently to absorb excess oil. Season with salt and pepper.

9 Re-season the soup as necessary, and serve garnished with a splash of cream, cilantro, and fried carrot shavings.

SERVES 6

2 medium (about 3 lb/1.4kg each) butternut squashes

3 tbsp peanut oil

1½ tsp sea salt

1¼ tsp pepper

1 cup/170g finely grated carrot

1 large onion, diced

1½ tsp ground cumin

2 cups/480ml low or no sodium chicken stock

½ cup/120ml cream

fresh cilantro (coriander), chopped, to garnish

For the fried carrot shavings:

1 cup/240ml peanut oil

1 carrot, shaved with a vegetable peeler

Sweet Potato Soup

Caroline Verschoor and her husband Jon Paul Saunier live in a Virginia farmhouse surrounded by rolling hills, pastures, animals, and the many friends of their two daughters, Sophie and Gwenael. The couple often host sleepovers and parties for the younger crowd. Caroline, who owns and runs her company, Ekster Antiques, from the huge barn on the property, knows how to stage memorable sets for those special occasions using furnishings and accessories from the ample stock of pieces she imports from her native Holland.

1 Cut all the vegetables into chunks.

2 Put the olive oil in a skillet (frying pan), add the vegetables and cook over medium heat until tender. Add the chicken stock and let simmer for 30 minutes. Purée with a stick blender.

3 Season with salt and pepper and serve in warmed soup bowls garnished with fresh cilantro.

SERVES 6

1 red onion, peeled

1½ red bell peppers, seeded

3 medium carrots, peeled

1 medium sweet potato, peeled

6 celery sticks

1 pint/½ liter chicken stock

1 tbsp olive oil

sea salt and ground black pepper

bunch of fresh cilantro (coriander), to garnish

Tips

For a thinner soup, add more chicken stock until you get the preferred consistency.

This recipe can easily be doubled.

Grilled Tartine with Eggs and Peppers

There is nothing quite as lovely as a picnic out in a field, especially when the fare is as simple and fresh as these little tartines made by Giampiero and Elizabeth Kirkpatrick. Cook the hard-boiled eggs and slice the peppers ahead of time and just add to hot off the grill crunchy bread.

1 Place the peppers, arugula, and spinach in a bowl, add 1 tbsp olive oil and toss. Set aside.

2 Brush both sides of the bread slices with the remaining olive oil. Grill over medium–high heat or fry in a skillet (frying pan) until golden and crisp.

3 Top each slice with the pepper, arugula, and spinach mixture. Add the slices of hard-cooked egg. Season with salt and pepper, garnish with a basil leaf, and eat while the bread is still warm and crisp.

SERVES 2

½ small yellow bell pepper, seeded and cut lengthwise into 1 inch/2.5cm strips

½ small red bell pepper, seeded and sliced lengthways into 1 inch/2.5cm strips

½ small orange bell pepper, seeded and sliced lengthways into 1 inch/2.5cm strips

4 arugula (rocket) leaves, stems removed

4 spinach leaves, stems removed

3 tbsp olive oil

2 thick slices multigrain bread

2 eggs, hard-cooked (hard-boiled), peeled and sliced

sea salt and ground black pepper

fresh basil leaves, to garnish

This is every cook's opinion—
no savory dish without an onion,
but lest your kissing should be spoiled
your onions must be fully boiled.

Jonathan Swift

chapter 2
main courses

Summer Tomato Tart

When she bought her farmhouse in New York State a few years ago, the first thing Anne Vitiello did was to set up a sizable garden plot. Now she prides herself on growing all the vegetables her family needs during the summer months. Her recipe for tomato tart is perfect for using up a glut of tomatoes—in fact, it tastes best when made with really ripe fruits, freshly picked off the vine.

1 Blanch 6 garlic cloves in a steamer or large pan of boiling water, refresh under cold, running water, drain, finely chop and set aside.

2 Make the pesto. Place the basil, parsley, and spinach in large plastic bag, pound with a meat pounder or other simple, heavy implement, until all the leaves are bruised.

3 Place the basil, parsley, and spinach mixture, blanched garlic, pignoli, olive oil, and salt in the bowl of a food processor (in batches if necessary). Process until almost smooth, stopping to scrape down as needed.

4 Transfer the mixture to a medium/large mixing bowl, add the roasted garlic and mash it into the pesto with a fork, stir in the Parmesan and Romano, and adjust the salt. Surplus pesto can be stored in the refrigerator for up to 1 week, if filmed with oil and/or covered with a sheet of plastic wrap (clingfilm) directly on the surface of the pesto.

5 Preheat the oven to 400°F/200°C/gas mark 6.

6 Roll out the dough for the tart(s) on a lightly floured surface to a thickness of ⅛ inch/3mm and use to line the tart pan(s). Crimp the edges.

7 Assemble the tart(s). Spread a layer of pesto on the bottom of the tart shell(s). Sprinkle half the grated cheese over the pesto. Layer tomatoes, alternating colors if possible, in a single but overlapping layer, to cover the surface with just a bit of pesto peeking through. Sprinkle with the remaining cheese and season with salt and pepper. Bake until the crust is golden brown, 45–55 minutes.

8 Transfer to a wire rack and cool for 20 minutes. Remove from the tart pan(s), slice, and serve warm.

SERVES 8

favorite pie crust dough to make one 10-inch/25cm or two 4 x 13-inch/10 x 33cm tart shells

1 cup/115g mild, grated cheese (fontina, mozzarella, or provolone)

2 lb/900g variety of fresh vine tomatoes, cored and sliced ¼ inch/5mm thick

sea salt and ground black pepper

For the pesto:

6 garlic cloves

8 cups packed/115g fresh basil leaves

½ cup packed/20g fresh flat leaf parsley

1½ cups packed/85g fresh baby spinach leaves

1 cup/140g pignoli (pine nuts)

1¾ cups /420ml extra-virgin olive oil

¼–½ tsp sea salt

6 garlic cloves, roasted

½ cup/50g freshly grated Parmesan

½ cup/50g freshly grated Romano cheese

Steak Salad

Summer is short-lived on the Illinois prairie. To make the most of what her garden provides, Jennifer Rizzo came up with this healthy, easy, and versatile salad. Switching from grain-fed to grass-fed beef from a local farm made it even healthier.

1 First make the croutons. Preheat the oven to 400°F/200°C/gas mark 6.

2 Over low heat, gently melt the butter in a pan. Turn off the heat, add the garlic, and let sit for a few minutes while you cut the bread into small bite-sized cubes.

3 Add the bread cubes to the pan and coat with the garlic butter. Spread the bread on a baking sheet that has been lined with parchment paper. Place the pan in the oven, checking every 3–5 minutes, stirring the croutons so they brown evenly. When they are slightly brown and crisp, remove from the oven and let cool.

4 Prepare the steak. Turn the oven to broil (grill). Cook the steak in a pan under the broiler (grill) until medium or to your taste. Remove from the heat and let rest in a covered pan for 5 minutes.

5 Meanwhile, toss the beets into the salad greens, add the croutons, and dress with your favorite salad dressing. Divide evenly on individual dinner plates.

6 Season the steak with salt and pepper, slice, and arrange over the salad.

SERVES 4

For the croutons:

1 stick/115g butter

2-3 garlic cloves, peeled and finely chopped

1 loaf French bread (day old or stale works better)

For the salad:

2 lb/900g grass-fed rib eye steaks

approximately 2–3 cups/50g baby salad greens per person.

4 pickled beets (beetroot), quartered

favorite salad dressing, to serve

sea salt and ground black pepper

Tips

Grass-fed steak can develop a stronger flavor the more well done it is.

Adjust cooking time according to personal preference (shorter for rare, longer for well done).

Variations:

Add goat cheese to the salad with the beets.

Substitute chicken for the steak, or replace with chickpeas to go vegetarian.

For a bit of sweetness, add ½ cup/50g cooked cranberries to a balsamic vinaigrette.

In summer, add a few sliced tomatoes and a bit of basil.

Vegetable Bread Pudding

Growing up in the shadow of her grandparents' restaurant "Wuerstle's Café" could only result in a love of food and cooking for Lizzie McGraw. From a young age Lizzie would follow her Gram around the kitchen. She learned to bake pies, especially lemon meringue, and cakes early on. She often helped with holiday meals, thanksgiving turkey with all the fixings being a favorite. Her Gram was a fan of experimenting with recipes, she loved to add caraway seeds to just about anything! Lizzie learned to not be shy about adding the ingredients she likes to her favorite recipes—why not add extra pecans, dried cherries, or blueberries to your favorite cake! Many of the dishes she enjoys making are variations of recipes she inherited from her Gram, Aunt Dottie, and other beloved relatives.

SERVES 4–6

1 large onion, diced

1 tbsp olive oil

4 cups/200g fresh spinach, cooked and strained

2 cups/500g ripe Roma tomatoes (or other small plum tomatoes), diced

1 baguette, cut into 1-inch/2.5cm thick slices

2 cups/450g thinly sliced cooked red potatoes

2 cups/225g shredded mozzarella cheese

1 cup/115g grated Parmesan

6 eggs

2 cups/480ml milk

1 tsp Tabasco sauce

sea salt and ground black pepper

1 Preheat the oven to 350°F/180°C/gas mark 4.

2 In a skillet (frying pan), sauté the onion in olive oil until tender. Add the spinach and tomatoes. Cook 1 minute more and remove from the heat.

3 In a 12-inch/30cm cast iron skillet or ovenproof dish, layer half of each: baguette slices, potatoes, and cheese, in that order. Top with all of the onion, tomatoes, and spinach mixture. Add the remaining baguette slices, potatoes, and cheese.

4 In a bowl, beat the eggs. Add the milk, Tabasco, and salt and pepper, and pour over the layered bread and vegetables in the skillet.

5 Bake, uncovered for 1 hour, or until a knife inserted in the center of the pudding comes out clean.

Fish in Salt Crust

Ed and Susie Beall's home is not your typical California home. Thanks to Ed's architect's skills and Susie's interior designer eye, you might as well be in a sprawling French farmhouse complete with a thriving vegetable garden and fruit trees. The Bealls' love of gardening began years ago when their sons were little. "We had four hungry kids to feed so growing food and cooking were priorities," Susie recalls. "To this day Ed and I still enjoy tending our garden and preparing meals together using our own vegetables, herbs, and fruit to enhance the recipes we create as well as those inherited from friends or collected on our travels."

1 Preheat the oven to 350°F/180°C/gas mark 4.

2 Rinse the fish under cold running water. Insert the sliced fennel, garlic, and lemon into the fish cavity. Add salt and pepper to taste. Set aside.

3 In a large bowl, mix the kosher salt with the egg white. Spread half of the egg/salt mixture onto a baking sheet. Lay the fish over the mixture, and top with remaining egg/salt mixture. Press the mixture to fully seal the fish. For a dramatic presentation, paint the crust with watercolor to mimic the fish before baking (the paint does not penetrate the salt crust).

4 Bake for 30 minutes. Remove fish from the oven and crack open the salt crust. The fish will be perfectly steamed, moist, and fragrant.

SERVES 4

1 whole snapper or other mild fish, about 5 lb/2.3kg, scaled, gutted, and cleaned, with head and tail on

1 fennel bulb, sliced thinly

3 garlic cloves, sliced thinly

1 lemon, sliced thinly

10 lb/5kg kosher salt or coarse sea salt

10 egg whites

sea salt and ground black pepper

wastercolor paints (optional)

Rotisserie Chicken

The secret to Susie and Ed Beall's tender chicken is two-fold. First, brining, one of the oldest and most powerful forms of seasoning, flavoring, and curing, increases moisture content in the chicken, and boosts the flavor of the meat. Second, a pan filled with wine and herbs releases aromatic fumes that further enhance the spit roasting process, one of the most ancient forms of grilling.

1 Remove the giblets and neck from the chicken's cavity. Rinse the chicken under cold running water. Pat dry and set aside in the refrigerator.

2 To make the brine, bring 2 cups/480ml water to a boil. Add the salt, sugar, lemon juice, garlic, and herbs. Simmer until the sugar is dissolved. Remove from the heat and let cool.

3 Put the chicken in a large sealable plastic bag, or a non-reactive container with a lid, add the cooled brine and more water to immerse the chicken. Refrigerate overnight.

4 Remove the chicken from the brine and rinse it thoroughly under cold running water. Pat the chicken dry with paper towels (kitchen paper).

5 To cook, tie the chicken with twine and tuck in the lemon slices and rosemary sprigs (1 of each on the chest and back of the chicken.) Thread the chicken onto the rotisserie spit. Set a pan filled with red wine and the bunch of rosemary over the hot grill and under the spit. Keep adding wine to the pan as it evaporates.

6 Baste the chicken with the melted butter and cook until the internal temperature reaches 160°F/71°C (until the juices run clear when the thigh is pierced with a sharp knife), approximately 1½ hours. Remove from the spit and let rest for 15 minutes before carving.

7 Serve with the reduced wine sauce.

SERVES 4

1 whole farm-raised chicken (5–6 lb/2.2–2.7kg)

1 lemon, sliced

2 sprigs fresh rosemary

½ bottle/350ml red wine, plus extra

1 generous bunch fresh rosemary

4 tbsp/50g butter, melted

For the brine:

2 cups/480ml water, plus extra water

¼ cup/4 tbsp salt

¼ cup/50g sugar

juice of 2 lemons

3 garlic cloves, smashed

1 tsp each fresh or dry thyme, rosemary, and parsley

Tip

Brining needs to be done at a temperature of 40°F/4°C or below. Never put the chicken in hot brine. Cool the brine in the refrigerator to speed up the cooling process if needed before adding the chicken.

Country Roast Pork

*Los Angeles is a long way from the Iowa prairie where Debra Hall
was born and raised but when she and her husband Klay moved
to California, she brought with her the memories and recipes from
her years on the farm where her family raised crops and livestock.
Her container garden overflowing with favorite herbs and
vegetables is also a fragrant reminder, though a much smaller
version, of the garden where, as a little girl, she would sneak out
and hide among rows of fresh peas, peeling them open and eating
them warm from the sun.*

*Debra and her four sisters learned to drive tractors, hay baling,
bottle feeding newborn lambs, and preparing down home meals
with their mom. "I still call it farm food," Debra says. "Sunday was
always a big family dinner. We would prep all day with mom and
the tantalizing aroma of roasting meat and vegetables filled the
house." Debra honors that long-cherished tradition by cooking one
of her mom's roast recipes for Klay and their two teenage boys,
Luke and Jack, every Sunday.*

1 Preheat the oven to 350°F/180°C/gas mark 4.

2 With a sharp knife, pierce the roast on all sides and insert the
shallots and sage into the slits. Season well with salt and pepper.

3 In a roasting pan, melt the butter with the olive oil on top of the
stove (hob) over medium–high heat until it begins to bubble. Add the
roast and quickly sear on both sides. Add the gooseberries just long
enough to sauté until golden, then remove them from the roasting pan
and set aside.

4 Transfer the pork to the preheated oven, add the onions, and roast for
about 1½ hours, or until a meat thermometer inserted in the thickest
part of the meat reaches 160°F/70°C.

5 Serve with the gooseberries and roasted vegetables.

SERVES 6

1 4 lb/1.8kg boneless pork roast
4 shallots, peeled and quartered
1 small bunch fresh sage
sea salt and ground black pepper
2 tbsp/25g butter
1 tbsp extra-virgin olive oil
a small handful of fresh gooseberries
a small handful of tiny onions, peeled

red cabbage confit, to serve (page 95)
braised fennel, to serve (page 96)
sautéed potatoes, to serve (page 97)

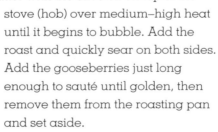

Zucchini-Goat Cheese Tart

SERVES 8

For the shortcrust pastry:

1¼ cups/140g unbleached all-purpose (plain) flour, plus extra if required

½ tsp sea salt

1 stick/115g unsalted butter, cut into small dice

3–4 tbsp ice water

butter, to grease pan

For the filling:

2–3 zucchini (courgettes)

1 tbsp extra-virgin olive oil

1 tsp Herbes de Provence

2 tbsp Dijon mustard

1 small log (about 4 oz/115g) chèvre (goat cheese)

4 eggs

1½ cups/360ml heavy (double) cream

sea salt and ground black pepper

From the tiny plot she began five years ago to today's garden overflowing with edibles of all sorts, Angela Reed's Illinois potager (vegetable garden) is a treasure trove of organic goodness. "I think I screamed with glee at the first fresh salad, even shed a tear at the first batch of crunchy, steamed green beans, and my heart still swoons at the taste of a juicy, velvety tomato, or the heady fragrance of a bunch of basil," she muses. It's no wonder that Angela is known for her fresh-from-the-garden recipes like her sun-ripened zucchini-goat cheese tart.

1 First make the tart shell. You can use an electric mixer or do it by hand. Mix the flour and salt together, add butter (mixing it in with your fingers until it becomes crumbly if you are doing it by hand). Slowly add water until a dough begins to form (do not overmix). It should hold together, but not be wet and sticky.

2 Put the dough inside a plastic bag and knead until smooth. Flatten the dough to a 6-inch/12-cm round and wrap with plastic wrap (clingfilm). Chill in the refrigerator for about 1 hour.

3 Remove dough from refrigerator and allow to soften slightly. Lightly butter a 9-inch/23cm quiche or tart pan (tin). I find the best way to do this is to smear a little butter on a paper towel (kitchen paper) and wipe the inside of the pan with it.

4 Roll out the dough on a lightly floured surface. Place it in the pan and trim the edges. Chill in the refrigerator for 30 minutes.

5 Make the filling. Preheat the oven to 400°F/200°C/gas mark 6. Cut the zucchini into ½-inch/1cm thick slices. In a skillet (frying pan), heat the olive oil over medium heat, add the zucchini and Herbes de Provence and sauté until slightly softened, or golden brown.

6 Remove the prepared pastry shell from the refrigerator, prick the inside all over with the tines of a fork, line with a parchment paper or aluminum foil, and fill with pie weights, rice, or

dried beans. This step is necessary to prevent the crust from bubbling up when you pre-bake it. Bake for 10 minutes, remove the parchment and weights or beans, and brush the mustard all over the pastry base. Bake for another 5–10 minutes, or until the shell is pale golden. Remove from the oven and transfer to a wire rack. Reduce the oven temperature to 350°F/180°C/gas mark 4. Cut the goat cheese into slices.

7 Assemble the tart. Mix together the eggs, cream, salt, and pepper. Arrange the zucchini in the crust, and place the goat cheese on top (you are not making a solid layer of goat cheese; there will be spaces in between each piece. Pour the egg mixture over all and bake for about 35 minutes, or until a knife inserted in the center of the tart comes out clean. Serve hot or warm, cut into wedges.

Grilled Chicken with Salad Leaves and Mandarin Oranges

For Sarah and Darius Anderson, grilling and salads are to summer what hearty soups and stews are to winter. Balsamic vinegar balances peppery arugula and radicchio's slight bitterness, and mandarins add a delicious sweet touch. The grilled chicken is the perfect complement to the flavorful greens in this quintessential summer salad.

1 Preheat the grill or a nonstick skillet (frying pan) to medium. Brush the chicken breasts on both sides using 1 tbsp olive oil. Season with salt and pepper.

2 Grill the chicken, turning once, until cooked through (2–3 minutes).

3 In a bowl, toss the arugula and radicchio with the remaining 3 tbsp olive oil and the vinegar. Add salt and pepper to taste.

4 Arrange the salad leaves on a large platter (or divide between 4 dinner plates). Slice each chicken breast and place over the salad. Garnish with the mandarin oranges.

SERVES 4

4 x 6oz/170g boneless, skinless chicken breasts

4 tbsp extra-virgin olive oil

2 generous bunches of arugula (rocket), stems removed

1 small head radicchio, leaves torn

1 tbsp balsamic vinegar

11 oz/300g can mandarin oranges, drained or same quantity fresh mandarin orange segments, to garnish

sea salt and ground black pepper

Slow-cooked Lamb Shanks

Spring comes slowly on the Illinois plain where Anne Marie, her husband Jason, and their six little children live the prairie lifestyle they love. Even when there is still a nip in the air, Anne Marie is quick to harvest the first offerings of the season. When she plans meals for her family she does not have to go far for inspiration. Right outside of her front door stands her potager already brimming with ruby red rhubarb, verdant lettuces, and an array of other tender edibles. This is where she grows not only her organic crops but health and harmony as well. For Anne Marie, cultivating her garden and home cooking go hand in hand with self-reliance and the deep connection between the food of the land, family, and traditions.

1 Preheat the oven to 325°F/160°C/gas mark 3.

2 Rinse the lamb shanks under cold water and pat dry.

3 In a heavy skillet (frying pan), heat 3 tbsp olive oil over medium–high heat and sauté the lamb shanks on all sides until golden brown.

4 Meanwhile, cut six 11 x 13-inch/28 x 33-cm lengths of aluminum foil to create a "roasting package."

5 Place 2 lamb shanks in each piece of foil and drizzle with olive oil. Add 2 sprigs of rosemary and thyme to each package and distribute the garlic evenly. Season with salt and pepper, cover with more aluminum foil, and wrap tightly to prevent the juices from escaping.

6 Place the foil-wrapped lamb shanks in a large roasting pan with a lid and roast for 3 hours. Reduce the oven temperature to 300°F/150°C/gas mark 2 and roast for one more hour. Remove from the oven and let rest for about 10 minutes.

7 Remove the foil and serve two lamb shanks over a scoop of white bean ragout.

Note: You can finish the lamb shanks over an open flame, preferably a wood-burning grill, or in a cast iron skillet (frying pan) to enhance them with a distinctively smoky and earthy flavor.

**SERVES 6
(2 SHANKS PER
PERSON)**

12 lamb shanks

3 tbsp extra-virgin olive oil, plus more for drizzling

12 sprigs fresh rosemary

12 sprigs fresh thyme

4 garlic cloves, peeled and chopped

sea salt and ground black pepper

White bean ragout (see page 88), to serve

Tri-Tip Roast

Maria Carr's mother, Trudy Farrier, came from a family of 11 kids and grew up on a cattle ranch. Her parents homesteaded in Montana where Maria's grandmother cooked on a wood stove until she was in her late nineties. It's no surprise that, in keeping with the family tradition, Maria learned to bake while living on the family farm. "I grew up with five brothers and five sisters and we shared chores. My main job was to make sure my brothers and dad were fed some sort of dessert every night," Trudy says. Today, Maria and her husband Thad and their five children live on a ranch in Northern California where, to the delight of her family, Maria not only puts her baking lessons to daily use but also cooks up many other hearty recipes she inherited from her grandma and her mom.

SERVES 4–6

tri-tip beef roast (see note), about 2½ lb/1.15kg
1 head garlic
sea salt and ground black pepper

1 Pierce the beef with a knife several times on each side of the roast and insert peeled garlic cloves into the openings. Season with salt and pepper.

2 Heat the grill on high heat. Sear both sides for 3 minutes each. Reduce the heat to medium and grill each side for 5 minutes.

3 Add salt and pepper throughout the cooking process (optional).

4 Remove from the heat, cover loosely with aluminum foil, and let stand for 10 minutes (for medium-rare) before slicing.

Note: Tri Tip is also known as triangle roast, bottom sirloin, butt, corner cut, knuckle cap, and aiguillette barone. A tri-tip roast averages between 1½–2½lb/685g–1.5kg.

Savory Grilled Lamb Chops

SERVES 4

2lb/900g rack of lamb (about 8 chops)
1 garlic clove
1 large fresh rosemary sprig
1 tbsp sea salt
1 tsp ground black pepper

Giampiero Kirkpatrick's grilled lamb chops prove that as with many things in life, simplicity equals good taste. A touch of garlic, a sprig of rosemary, and a bit of salt and pepper combined into a gentle rub is all it takes to complement the delicate texture of the chops.

1 Allow the lamb to come to room temperature. Trim the fat to expose 1–1½ inches/2.5–3cm of bones and about ⅛ inch/3mm of fat. Partially cut through the rack of lamb along the bones, making sure to leave it connected at the bottom.

2 In a bowl, finely chop the garlic and rosemary, add the salt and pepper and mix well. Rub the seasoned herb mixture over the lamb, including the cut area.

3 Set the prepared lamb on a kettle grill over high heat. Close the cover. Grill on each side for 10–15 minutes, or according to personal level of doneness (a medium-rare rack of lamb has an internal temperature of around 130°F/55°C). If using a different type of grill, follow instructions.

4 Once the rack has reached the desired temperature, remove from the heat, and set aside. Cover loosely with foil and let rest for 10–20 minutes before serving.

Cassoulet

This simple rustic stew is a satisfying antidote for wintry days, and a wonderful way to use leftover poultry and meats. As Susie Beall can attest, like all great stews, it's even better reheated.

1 Preheat the oven to 350°F/180°C/gas mark 4.

2 Drain the beans and rinse. Place in a bowl with the lemon juice. Add the meat, sausage, and poultry. Stir in the tomato paste, garlic, and duck fat.

3 Put the mixture into 6 ramekins, or in a 1-quart/1-liter buttered Dutch oven (casserole), and add enough chicken stock to bring the mixture almost to the top.

4 Sprinkle with bread crumbs, add the parsley, and drizzle with melted butter.

5 Bake ramekins for 30 minutes; bake the Dutch oven for 45 minutes, or until browned and bubbly.

SERVES 6–8

15-oz/420g can small white beans (cannellini beans)

juice of 1 lemon

2 cups/about 500g mixture of leftover meats and poultry (traditionally pork, sausage, and duck but any combination will work)

2 tbsp tomato paste (purée)

4 garlic cloves, finely chopped

⅓ cup/5 tbsp duck fat

1 cup/240ml chicken stock

2 cups/225g bread crumbs

½ cup/20g chopped fresh flat-leaf parsley

1 tbsp butter, melted

Harvest Beef Stew

When planning a party menu, Caroline Verschoor always tries to prepare dishes ahead of time. "It's convenient because I don't have to spend the day cooking up a storm," she says. "All I have to do is reheat and let simmer, which allows the flavors to blend even more." This technique works particularly well for this stew. Not only is the meat fork-tender, but the aroma wafting from the kitchen imbues the whole house with a distinct fall flavor.

1 In a large resealable plastic bag combine the flour, pepper, and salt. Add the meat to the bag, one third at a time, and shake to coat with flour.

2 In a 8-quart/8-liter Dutch oven (casserole), heat the olive oil and brown the beef with the garlic, one third at a time, for 5–6 minutes or until the beef is colored all over. Drain off any fat.

3 Return all the beef to the Dutch oven. Stir in the beef stock, red wine, and water, and add sage leaves. Bring to a boil; reduce heat, cover and simmer for 1½ hours.

4 Stir in the potatoes, sweet potatoes, onions, and carrots. Return to boiling; reduce heat. Cover and simmer for 15–20 minutes or until vegetables are tender. Discard the sage leaves. Add the corn and peas, stir gently, and let simmer for about 10 minutes.

5 To serve, ladle the hot stew into warmed bowls. If desired, top each with a dollop of sour cream.

SERVES 10–12

½ cup/55g all-purpose (plain) flour

1 tsp ground black pepper

½ tsp sea salt

3 lb/1.35kg boneless beef chuck roast (stewing beef), cut into ¾-inch/2-cm cubes

3 tbsp olive oil

3 garlic cloves, finely chopped

5¼ cups/1.2 liters beef stock

1 pint/480ml dry red wine

1 cup/240ml water

4 fresh sage leaves

2 lb/900g potatoes, peeled and cubed

1 lb/450g sweet potatoes, peeled and cubed

1 lb/450g fresh peeled pearl (pickling) onions or frozen small whole onions

1 lb/450g fresh peeled baby carrots or frozen baby carrots

8 oz/225g can corn (sweetcorn), drained, or frozen corn

1 lb/450g fresh or frozen peas

Sour cream, to garnish (optional)

Venison Stroganoff

Jason Shepherd gives the classic Stroganoff dish a flavorful twist with venison. "If not prepared properly, the meat can be tough due to its low fat content," he notes. "By cubing it finely, and then cooking it a long time in stock and wine, it becomes tender and aromatic. We like to think of venison as the ultimate grass-fed meat!"

SERVES 8

3 tbsp/40g butter (ideally European-style)

2 large carrots, peeled and diced

2 medium onions, peeled and diced

5 garlic cloves, peeled and finely chopped

1 tbsp sea salt

1 tsp pepper

3 lb/1.4kg cubed venison

6 oz/170g baby bella (portobello) mushrooms, cut in half

2 tsp dried thyme

2 cups/480ml red wine (cabernet sauvignon is s good option)

1 quart/1 liter chicken stock (homemade is best)

2 beef bouillon cubes, dissolved in the stock

12 oz/340g egg noodles

2 tbsp/30g butter (ideally European-style)

1 lb/450g cream cheese

1 cup/225g sour cream

fresh flat-leaf parsley, chopped, for garnish

1 Preheat the oven to 225°F/110°C/gas mark ¼.

2 In a Dutch oven (casserole), add the first 3 tbsp/40g butter, diced carrots, onions, garlic, pinch of salt, and 1 tsp pepper, and cook for 10 minutes on medium heat. Add the venison and cook until juices are rendered. Add the mushrooms and thyme and continue cooking the meat until the juices have reduced. Deglaze with half the red wine, and continue cooking until the wine evaporates.

3 Add 2–3 cups/480–720ml of stock (enough to cover the meat), cover the pot, and place in the preheated oven. Cook for 8 hours.

4 Remove pot from oven, put back on stove (hob) over medium heat, and cook until all juices have evaporated. Or, prior to removing from oven, increase heat to 350°F/180°C/gas mark 4, remove lid and let cook until juices have evaporated.

5 Deglaze a second time with the remaining wine and stock. Reduce liquid by one-third over medium heat.

6 Meanwhile, cook the egg noodles as per pack directions, drain, return to the pot, and add the remaining 2 tbsp/30g butter. Keep warm.

7 Once the wine has reduced, stir the cream cheese and sour cream into the venison. Heat gently.

8 Serve the stroganoff over the egg noodles, garnished with the parsley.

Meatloaf Cake

SERVES 6–8

1 tbsp extra-virgin olive oil

1 medium onion, chopped

3 garlic cloves, finely chopped

1 lb/450g ground (minced) beef

1 lb/450g sweet Italian sausage, casing removed

½ tsp fresh thyme leaves

2 tbsp Dijon mustard

2 tbsp wholegrain mustard

2 tbsp Worcestershire sauce

½ tsp Tabasco sauce

1 cup/240ml milk

⅔ cup/70g crushed saltine crackers (salted plain crackers)

¼ cup/15g fresh flat-leaf parsley

2 eggs, beaten

peas, sliced mushrooms, and sliced onions, for garnish (optional)

When it comes to "making do," it's hard to beat the versatility and affordability of meatloaf. Using inexpensive meats is a sure way to stretch one's food budget while serving a hearty meal. For a twist on tradition, Susie Beall uses a bundt cake pan instead of the usual loaf pan. Whether served hot as a main course, or sliced cold for a sandwich, meatloaf remains one of Susie's "go to" recipes.

1 Preheat the oven to 350°F/180°C/gas mark 4.

2 Heat the olive oil in a pan over medium heat. Sauté the onion and garlic until golden. Set aside.

3 In a large bowl or mixer, combine the beef, sausage, thyme, mustards, Worcestershire sauce, Tabasco, milk, crackers, parsley, onion and garlic, and beaten eggs. Mix well.

4 Put the mixture in an ungreased 10-inch/25cm bundt cake pan (fluted cake tin) and bake at 350°F/180°C/gas mark 4 for 1 hour, or until a meat thermometer reads 160°F/71°C. Serve hot or cold, garnished with peas, mushrooms, and onions, if liked.

Salmon with Herb Dressing

Lulu Tapp knows that wild salmon is a much better option than the farm-raised type, as it does not contain any food coloring or additives. The accompanying herb and honey dressing gets its summery zest from lemon juice, its kick from a touch of garlic, and its heat from a hint of Jalapeno.

1 First make the herb dressing: put the garlic and jalapeno pepper in a food processor and pulse until finely chopped.

2 Add the herbs, lemon juice, and honey. With the food processor running, drizzle in the oil slowly. Season with salt and pepper.

3 Make the tomato topping: gently toss the grape tomatoes, ¼ cup/60ml olive oil, chopped chives, and lemon juice together in a bowl. Season with salt and pepper and set aside.

4 Prepare the salmon. Heat a grill or grill pan over high heat. Drizzle each salmon fillet with olive oil and season with salt and pepper. Spray the grill with vegetable oil.

5 Add the salmon to the hot grill. Sear each side for 4 minutes. (Do not try to move it too soon or it will stick.) Loosen gently with tongs, and set on plates.

6 Spread the herb dressing around the fish and dollop the tomato mixture on top. Garnish with a few grape tomatoes, and little sprigs of fresh dill.

SERVES 2

2 x 6oz /170g thick salmon fillets

extra-virgin olive oil, to drizzle

vegetable oil for the grill

few grape (baby plum) tomatoes, halved, to garnish

fresh dill sprigs, to garnish

For the herb dressing:

1 medium garlic clove

¼ small Jalapeno pepper, diced

1 cup/50g fresh cilantro (coriander)

½ cup/25g fresh mint

¼ cup/10g fresh flat-leaf parsley

juice of 1 lemon

1 tbsp honey

¾ cup/180ml extra-virgin olive oil

sea salt and ground black pepper

For the tomato topping:

1 cup/170g grape (baby plum) tomatoes, halved

¼ cup/60ml extra-virgin olive oil

2 tbsp chopped fresh chives

juice of ½ lemon

Mussels in Pine Needles

Though the Bealls share equal time in the kitchen, some dishes are Ed's specialty, among which is this age-old mussels recipe. Grilling has been in existence since man discovered fire and "eclade" is one of the most distinctive styles of barbecuing. This simple method consists of cooking mussels under blazing dry pine needles. The smoky flavor imparted by the pine needles is equal to none, and the mussels are cooked to perfection in a heartbeat.

SERVES 2

2 lb/900g black mussels, soaked and beards removed
2 quarts/2 liters dried pine needles
lemon butter or tomato salsa, to serve

1 To clean the mussels, scrub them well under cold running water. Discard any mussels that don't have tightly closed shells and those with cracked shells. Pull out and discard any clumps of black, beard like string from the hinges of the mussels.

2 Place the mussels in a wok or large metal bowl on top of a grate in a barbecue pit.

3 Cover with 4 inches/10cm dried pine needles and set the needles on fire. When the needles have turned to ash, the mussels will be cooked.

4 Remove the mussels from the heat and put into two bowls. Spoon lemon butter or tomato salsa over the open mussels. Serve hot. (Do not eat any mussels with closed shells.)

Pasta with Meat Gravy

SERVES 8

4 tbsp extra-virgin olive oil
1 large onion, peeled and diced
2–3 tbsp finely chopped garlic
1½ lb/675g ground (minced) beef
15-oz/420g can tomato sauce (passata)
12-oz/340g can tomato paste (purée)
2 cups/480ml water
1 tbsp dried parsley
2 tbsp dried oregano
1 tsp sugar
sea salt and ground black pepper
favorite pasta, to serve

Italians refer to spaghetti sauce as "gravy," which is thicker, meatier, and much tastier than traditional store-bought sauce. Tracey Leber grew up on her grandmother Ann Desideri's homemade sauce. "My grandma was not Italian, but my grandfather was 100 per cent, and grandma made a lot of traditional Italian dishes to please him. I have been making this recipe since I was in high school and think of her every single time I make it."

1 Heat 2 tbsp olive oil in a heavy stock pot over medium-high heat. Once the oil is hot, add the onion and cook until soft. Reduce heat to medium, add the garlic, and cook for 3 minutes.

2 Meanwhile, add the remaining olive oil to another pan and brown the beef.

3 Add the tomato sauce, tomato paste, water, parsley, oregano, and sugar to the onion mixture.

4 Drain the beef and add to the tomato sauce. Add salt and pepper to taste, and bring to a boil. Simmer over low heat for 1½ hours stirring occasionally. Serve with your favorite pasta.

Roasted Spaghetti Squash with Shaved Parmesan

Low on carbs and high in nutrients, spaghetti squash is a tasty substitute for pasta and a pleasurable way to add more vegetables to a healthy diet. Jason Shepherd tops it with a bit of olive oil and fresh Parmesan for added savor. This dish is not only easy to prepare, but one forkful and you will never miss the pasta.

SERVES 4

1 medium–large spaghetti squash
2 tbsp extra-virgin olive oil
sea salt and ground black pepper
Parmesan cheese, to garnish

1 Preheat the oven to 350°F/180°C/gas mark 4.

2 Cut the spaghetti squash in half lengthwise and scoop out the seeds.

3 Brush olive oil onto the flesh and season liberally with salt and pepper.

4 Place flesh-side down on a baking sheet and roast for 1 hour.

5 Remove from the oven and let cool long enough to handle. With a fork, scrape out the flesh (it will resemble spaghetti).

6 Plate the spaghetti squash, drizzle with additional olive oil, if desired, and season with pepper to taste. Garnish with shavings of fresh Parmesan. Serve hot.

Maple-Honey-Walnut Chicken

SERVES 4–6

3–4 lb/1.35–1.8kg farm-raised chicken

2⅞ tbsp/40g unsalted butter

1 tsp fine sea salt

1 tbsp coarse sea salt

1 cup/115g walnut pieces

sea salt and ground black pepper

For the glaze:

2 tbsp honey

2 tbsp maple syrup

1 tbsp balsamic vinegar

1 tsp chili powder

A plump maple-roasted chicken was a traditional meal for my family every Sunday night during the long winters on the Canadian prairie. My children were raised on this comforting recipe. And, now that my boys are grown and living far away, I still make it for myself and share it with my cats every Sunday. The scent of maple syrup wafting through the house never fails to conjure up those happy, but long ago days when we gathered around the kitchen table on starlit nights shining brightly over the still, frozen land. Every bite of this succulent dish comes with a side of sweet nostalgia.

1 Preheat the oven to 475°F/240°C/gas mark 9.

2 Rinse the chicken, pat dry with paper towels (kitchen paper) inside and out. Sprinkle the cavity with salt and pepper.

3 To make the glaze, mix the honey, maple syrup, vinegar, and chili powder in a small bowl, stirring well. Add more maple syrup or honey if you like a sweeter taste or more balsamic vinegar and chili powder for a spicier result. Whichever way your taste buds dictate, only add the chosen ingredients a little at a time until you get the preferred balance. Set aside.

4 In a small skillet (frying pan) melt 2 tbsp/30g butter over low heat (do not let it burn). Brush the chicken on all sides with the melted butter. Season the outside of the chicken with the coarse sea salt—this will make the skin crisper.

5 Set the chicken, breast side down, in a roasting pan. Place it on a rack in the center of the preheated oven for about 15 minutes. Reduce the temperature to 450°F/230°C/gas mark 8, and continue roasting for another 15 minutes. Baste the chicken with the pan drippings, reduce heat to 425°F/220°C/gas mark 7, and continue roasting until the internal temperature of the chicken reaches 180°F/82°C.

6 Meanwhile, put the walnut pieces in a saucepan with the remaining ½ tbsp/10g butter and cook over low–medium heat until the walnuts look golden. Remove from the heat and set aside.

7 Combine the drippings from the pan with the honey-maple mixture in a bowl, add the walnuts, and pour over the chicken. Return the pan to the oven and broil (grill) for about 5 minutes, watching carefully so it does not burn.

8 Let the chicken rest for 15 minutes on a cutting board before carving and serving.

Pot Roast with Root Vegetables

SERVES 6–8

3–4 lb/1.4–1.8kg boneless sirloin tip or beef tenderloin roast (joint), tied

sea salt and ground black pepper

roasted root vegetables, to serve (see page 101)

For the marinade:

6 garlic cloves

3 tbsp fresh rosemary leaves

4 tbsp olive oil

4 tbsp canola (rapeseed) oil, plus additional for browning the roast

4 tbsp Worcestershire sauce

2 tbsp fresh thyme leaves

A Sunday roast (beef, pork, or lamb) served for lunch was a British custom that was passed down through the generations and carried over to America. At Barbara and Everett Jacksier's Foxwood Farm, roasted vegetables accompanying a succulent roast take on seasonal flair prepared with just-picked herbs (see page 101). Sometimes Barbara is asked why she inserts the meat thermometer 20 minutes after the beef goes into the oven, and she says there is no reason except that it's the way her mother always does it!

1 Remove the beef from refrigerator and place it in a baking pan or deep dish. Sprinkle liberally with salt and pepper.

2 Mix all marinade ingredients together and coat the beef on all sides. Let stand at room temperature for 1 hour.

3 Preheat the oven to 450°F/230°C/gas mark 8.

4 Meanwhile, heat a few tablespoons of oil in a heavy ovenproof pan on top of the stove (hob). Reserving the marinade, transfer the beef to the pan and brown on all sides, about 8–10 minutes. Turn off the heat and pour the reserved marinade on the beef.

5 Place the beef in the preheated oven. After 20 minutes, turn the beef and insert a meat thermometer. When the meat thermometer reads 130°F/55°C, remove the meat from the oven and let it rest for 10–15 minutes.

6 When ready to serve, remove the string and slice. Transfer slices to a large serving platter and surround with roasted root vegetables (see page 101).

Can the garden afford any thing more delightful to view than those forests of asparagus, artichokes, lettuce, pease, beans and other legumes and edulous plants so different in colour and of such various shapes, rising at it were from the dead and piercing the ground in so many thousand places as they do, courting the admiration or requiring the care of the diligent Gardiner.

Stephen Switzer, The Practical Gardener, 1727

chapter 3
side dishes

Asparagus with Hollandaise Sauce

For Anne Marie, harvesting her own vegetables and cooking for her family are but two of many pleasures. She prides herself in serving healthy and flavorful dishes, like just-picked asparagus with the buttery goodness, and gentle lemony tang of hollandaise. The fresh eggs from her chickens make the classic sauce even more flavorful.

1 Cut the raw end of the asparagus spears and wash under cold water. Place in a skillet (frying pan) with ½ cup/120ml cold water and let simmer on medium–high heat for about 5 minutes—do not overcook. Cook the asparagus until they turn bright green so that they will remain crisp, but tender.

2 Remove from the heat, drain, and run under cold water to retain the bright green color and stop the cooking process. Set aside if not serving immediately.

3 Quickly warm the asparagus in a skillet just enough to get them hot, before serving.

4 Make the hollandaise: stir the egg yolks with the lemon juice in a heavy pan, keeping the heat on low and stirring constantly. Add half the butter and stir constantly until melted. Add the remaining butter, and again, stir constantly until melted, and the sauce is beginning to thicken. Serve at once over the hot asparagus.

SERVES 4–6

24 fresh asparagus spears
½ cup/120ml water

For the hollandaise sauce:

2 egg yolks
2 tbsp fresh lemon juice
1 stick/115g very cold butter

Homemade Fettuccine

SERVES 6–8

For spinach pasta:

9 oz/250g fresh spinach, cut up and sautéed quickly to wilt or 10 oz/280g pack frozen leaf spinach thawed

3 cups/340g unbleached organic all-purpose (plain) flour

1 tsp sea salt

2 large free-range eggs

1–2 tbsp water, if needed

1 tbsp extra-virgin olive oil

small bunch of fresh Italian or flat-leaf parsley

sea salt and ground black pepper

freshly grated Romano cheese, optional

A true believer in homegrown, homemade, and home cooked, Anne Marie even makes her own pasta. She not only prefers the resulting fresh taste and velvety texture, but enjoys the process of kneading the dough, rolling it out, and cutting it into strips as well. The other advantage, she says, is that you can flavor it to suit your taste, may it be spinach, tomato, squash, or favorite herbs.

1 Using a food processor, pulse the spinach, flour, and salt until well combined.

2 In a small bowl, beat the eggs with a fork. With the processor running, slowly pour the beaten eggs in the feed tube until the mixture resembles coarse meal—about 1 minute only—if too dry, add the water.

3 Turn the dough onto a work surface and knead until smooth and elastic, about 6–8 minutes. Wrap in plastic wrap (clingfilm) and refrigerate for 30 minutes.

4 Unwrap the dough and cut into 12 pieces. Using a pasta machine,

pass it through the machine on the widest setting and continue this process 7 more times until all the edges are smooth. Continue this process, each time using a smaller setting until the pasta is ⅛ inch/ 3mm thick.

5 Place flattened sheets on a dish cloth and let dry for 8 minutes. If sticky, sprinkle a bit of flour over the resting dough.

6 Start water boiling in a large stockpot at least three-quarters full of fresh cold water, add a pinch of salt and 1 tbsp olive oil.

7 Feed sheets of dough through the ¼ inch/5mm cutter of the pasta machine. After each sheet is cut into fettuccine, place between flour dusted parchment paper. When all the dough is fed through, place into boiling water and cook for approximately 6–8 minutes for al dente, longer if you prefer the pasta more tender.

8 Toss the pasta with the fresh chopped parsley, and salt and pepper. Drizzle with a little olive oil and freshly grated Romano cheese (optional).

Variation:
For tomato pasta, add 12 oz/340g fresh, finely chopped tomato instead of spinach

SERVES 6–8

1 cup/225g fresh or frozen peas, blanched or lightly steamed

2 tbsp extra-virgin olive oil

1 large or 2 medium yellow onions, chopped

½ tsp chili powder

½ tsp ground cumin

½ tsp ground coriander

½ tsp saffron threads

½ tsp salt

¼–½ tsp cayenne pepper (optional)

1 cup/240ml chicken stock

2 lb/900g parsnips, peeled and cut into ½-inch/1-cm rounds at the thin end, and ½-inch/1-cm dice at the thick end

⅓–1 cup/75–240ml canned coconut milk (according to personal taste)

To serve:

rice, quinoa, or couscous (optional)

½ cup/85g roasted bell peppers, cut into thin strips

½ cup/50g roasted unsalted peanuts, chopped

1 sprig fresh mint, half coarsely chopped and half intact

Parsnip Curry

For Anne Vitiello, the first frost signals the time to harvest her parsnips and make one of her favorite seasonal dishes. She enhances the root vegetable's inherent notes of honey and butterscotch with the subtle accents of spices.

1 Place the peas in a pan with just enough water to cover. Cook over medium heat for 2–3 minutes. Drain and set aside.

2 Sauté the onion in olive oil over medium–high heat in a large pan until pale golden and translucent. A little golden brown color on the edges is fine too, and makes a sweeter stew.

3 Add all the spices to the pan, stir, and cook for 1–2 minutes, until well-blended and fragrant.

4 Add the chicken stock and parsnips, bring to a boil, then cover and simmer over low heat for 10–15 minutes until the parsnips are tender, but not mushy.

5 Add ⅓ cup/75ml coconut milk, and adjust quantity until preferred color/taste is achieved. The sauce should be fairly thick.

6 Serve in a bowl, or over rice, quinoa, or couscous, topped with roasted bell peppers, chopped peanuts, and fresh mint.

Sautéed Fiddleheads

Anne Vitiello knows spring has arrived the moment the gleaming, tight green coils of still-unfurled leaves of the young ostrich ferns huddled under trees bordering her farm appear. Their availability is short-lived and Anne is quick to harvest them. The delicate wild flavor and delightful texture of the tiny curled spirals of the fiddleheads—so named because they mimic the end of a violin—provide a rare treat as an appetizer or a side dish.

1 Trim any brown edges from the fiddlehead stems, and rub off any browned bits on the curled fronds. Rinse under cold, running water and dry thoroughly.

2 Heat the butter and olive oil over medium–high heat, and when the foam subsides, add the fiddleheads. Increase heat to high.

3 Sauté until the exterior is seared, approximately 1–3 minutes. Add the garlic and sauté until fragrant and softened, another minute or two. Add the wine.

4 After the wine is absorbed/burned off, reduce heat to medium, and cook for another 2–3 minutes, testing for tenderness with the tip of a good paring knife.

5 Serve hot with crusty bread.

SERVES 2–6 (i.e. 2 very hungry people in possession of a good crusty loaf of bread, or appetizers for up to 6 people)

1 lb/450g fresh fiddleheads

3 tbsp/40g butter

1 tbsp extra-virgin olive oil

3–5 garlic cloves, finely chopped

⅔ cup/150ml white wine

sea salt and ground black pepper

loaf of crusty bread, to serve

Tip

Be sure to choose only very green, tightly coiled fiddleheads.

White Bean Ragout

Eaten on its own with chunks of crusty bread, or as a companion to lamb (see page 54) or pork, Anne Marie's white bean ragout is as versatile as it is satisfying, especially on a winter day when the cold wind blows and the snow blankets the Illinois prairie.

1 Peel and chop the carrots and onion, chop the celery and the tomatoes, making sure all the chopped vegetables are close in size.

2 Heat the olive oil in a 4-quart/4-liter pan, add all the chopped vegetables and cook on medium heat for about 5 minutes—do not brown. Add the garlic, two generous pinches of salt and pepper, and the Herbes de Provence, stirring constantly. Add the chicken stock, and fold in the beans (do not crush them), and simmer the vegetables over low heat for about 10–15 minutes. When the carrots are fork-tender, the vegetables are done.

3 Chop the parsley and add to the cooked vegetables, being careful not to crush the beans. Serve hot, on its own, or with roasted meat, or crusty bread.

SERVES 6

3 carrots

1 large onion

2 celery sticks

2 ripe tomatoes

3 tbsp extra-virgin olive oil

3 garlic cloves, chopped

½ tsp Herbes de Provence

1 quart/1 liter chicken stock

24 oz/675g white cannellini beans (if using canned beans, drain first)

1 large bunch fresh parsley

sea salt and ground black pepper

Grilled Asparagus

Harbinger of spring, fleshy, green grilled asparagus spears are delectable when infused with olive oil, and is Maria Carr's preferred cooking method because it brings forth their earthy flavor.

1 Wash and trim the asparagus. If the stalks are thick, they will need to be peeled as well.

2 Set the prepared asparagus in a baking dish and drizzle with olive oil until well-coated. Season with salt and pepper.

3 Place the seasoned asparagus in an electric grill or skillet (frying pan) set over high heat. Sear for 1 minute on each side. Reduce heat to medium, and cook for 3 minutes on each side, until fork tender, but not soft.

SERVES 4–6

2 lb/900g asparagus
extra-virgin olive oil
sea salt and ground black pepper

Lost Trails Chunky Mashed Potatoes

After a day working on the ranch, Maria Carr knows her brood needs plenty of nourishment. These chunky and chewy mashed potatoes—cooked with the skins on to preserve valuable nutrients—are always a favorite whatever the season.

1 Cut the potatoes in quarters. In a large pan filled with enough water to completely cover the potatoes, boil the potatoes for 20 minutes, or until tender.

2 Drain the water and put the potatoes into the bowl of an electric mixer. Beat on low for about a minute. Add the melted butter, beat in the cream cheese, then add the milk. Season with salt and pepper and beat until creamy. Serve hot.

SERVES 4–6

6 Yukon Gold, Maris Piper, or other large waxy potatoes, skin on
½ cup/115g cream cheese
1 stick/115g butter, melted
¼ cup/60ml milk
sea salt and ground black pepper

Kale Chips

Unlike many kids, Anne Vitiello's children are quite fond of kale. In fact, they even consider it a treat. But that's because Anne's quick and easy recipe turns the hearty, healthy winter green into crunchy chips that they can't get enough of, whether she serves them as a snack, or with a main course.

1 Preheat the oven to 300°F/150°C/gas mark 2. Place the oven racks just above and below the center of the oven. Line 2 baking sheets with parchment paper or silicon mats.

2 Remove kale stems, and tear the leaves into bite-size pieces.

3 Rinse the kale in a salad spinner and spin thoroughly. Remove from the spinner and dry by blotting with paper towels (kitchen paper) or a clean dish cloth.

4 Toss the kale with olive oil, and spread on the prepared baking sheets in a single layer. Sprinkle over the salt and spices. Bake for 10 minutes. Switch baking sheets by moving the top one to the bottom and vice versa; bake for approximately 10 more minutes.

5 Check the kale. If still soft, bake for another 5–10 minutes, but watch carefully. As soon as the kale begins to brown, remove from the oven.

6 Let cool, and serve immediately. Do not refrigerate. If the chips grow soggy, gently re-bake just enough to crisp up again.

SERVES 4

large bunch of kale, curly or straight

1½ tbsp extra-virgin olive oil

1–2 tsp finely ground sea salt

½ tsp cayenne pepper (optional)

1 tbsp smoked paprika

Flame-roasted Red Bell Peppers

6 firm, ripe red bell peppers
2 heads peeled garlic
juice of 1 lemon

Cooking peppers on an open flame is a sure way to enhance them with a smoky flavor while keeping them tender inside. Once cooled, the skin is easily removed to reveal the pepper's velvety texture.

1 Turn the flame on a gas stove (hob) to medium-low, or the correct height in order to have the most flame-to-pepper contact, and cook each red pepper directly on the stove top, rotating gently with tongs until all sides are well-blackened but the peppers are not cooked to the point of leaking. Alternatively, cook them on a grill.

2 Remove from the heat, and place the peppers in a salad spinner while they are cooling for up to an hour or so, letting them self-steam so as to ease removal of skins. Have two bowls ready, one small and one medium/large.

3 Skin and slice the peppers as follows: hold a pepper over the small bowl, pull it open, and allow the juices to leak into the bowl. Peel and discard the skins and seeds. (A few bits of blackened peel or seeds remaining is okay.) Save the juices.

4 Using a cutting board with a trough to catch any additional juice, slice the peppers into thin strips. Add these juices to the small bowl.

5 Place the sliced peppers in the large bowl, together with the garlic and lemon juice.

6 Using a fine mesh sieve lined with cheesecloth (muslin), pour the saved juices through the sieve into the large bowl, over the sliced peppers. Toss to mix all ingredients and coat the peppers well.

7 Cover tightly and leave the garlic to infuse the peppers for up to one week. After a week, remove and discard the garlic. Continue to store the peppers, refrigerated, for up to 3 weeks. They may also be sealed in mason (Kilner) jars, but not frozen.

Roasted Butternut Squash, Pear, and Walnut Salad

SERVES 8–10

1 medium butternut squash (1½–2 lb/
675–900g)

8 oz/225g mixed baby salad leaves

½ cup/15g arugula (rocket)

½ cup/55g radicchio, leaves torn into bite-
size pieces

2 small ripe red pears, cored and sliced

1 cup/115g cheddar cheese, shaved

½ cup/55g walnuts, chopped

For the dressing:

½ cup/120ml olive oil

⅓ cup/75ml balsamic vinegar

4 tablespoons honey

¼ tsp sea salt

1 tsp brown sugar

⅛ tsp ground allspice

ground black pepper, to taste

*Butternut squashes are plentiful in fall and Caroline
Verschoor picks hers from a neighboring farm that also
supplies a variety of greens and pumpkins. A trip to the
farm is a family affair as the girls join in to help gather
the goods. This salad is another seasonal dish that can
be prepared ahead of time. Only the pears, nuts, cheese,
and dressing need to be added just before serving.*

1 Preheat the oven to 425°F/220°C/gas mark 7.

2 Peel the squash, cut it in half, and remove the seeds.
Cut each half into 1-inch/2.5-cm cubes. Arrange in a
shallow roasting pan. Roast uncovered for 15 minutes.

3 For the dressing, in a small bowl whisk together the oil,
vinegar, honey, salt, sugar, allspice, and pepper until well
combined.

4 Drizzle 4 tbsp of the dressing over the partially baked
squash; toss to coat. Roast the squash for 5–10 minutes
more or until tender; cool in the pan on a wire rack for
about 20 minutes. Reduce the oven temperature to
350°F/180°C/gas mark 4.

5 Bake the walnuts in the oven
in a shallow roasting pan for
about 10 minutes or until
toasted. Cool slightly.

6 To assemble, arrange mixed
salad leaves, radicchio and
arugula on a large serving
platter. Top with the pear slices,
cheese, and squash cubes.
Drizzle remaining dressing
over the salad. Garnish with
the toasted walnuts.

Red Cabbage Confit

As a child, Debra Hall spent many summers helping her grandma in the kitchen. Her red cabbage confit is one of many recipes paying tribute to her grandma's legacy.

1 Put the cabbage in a large pot. Add enough water to completely cover the cabbage and bring to a boil over medium–high heat. Let boil for about 5 minutes, then reduce the heat to medium.

2 Add the wine, vinegar, sugar, butter, and salt and pepper. Reduce heat to medium-low and continue cooking until the cabbage is tender.

3 As the liquid is absorbed, add more water, vinegar, and sugar until the cabbage's balance of tartness and sweetness meets with your taste preference. The longer the cabbage is cooked, the better the results. Even once fully cooked it can remain on low heat as this will enhance both flavor and texture. Just keep adding a little water, vinegar, and sugar so that it will not dry up. This is one dish that also benefits from reheating, so make plenty for a second day.

SERVES 6

2 lb/900g red cabbage, thinly sliced

1 cup/240ml red wine

¼ cup/60ml red wine vinegar, plus additional to taste

4 tbsp sugar, plus additional to taste

3 tbsp/40g butter

sea salt and ground black pepper

Braised Fennel

Whether used raw in salads, or braised and served as an accompaniment, crunchy, and with a slight taste of licorice, fennel adds a refreshing, flavorful contribution to many dishes. Debra Hall pairs it with a pork roast, just like her mom used to do (see page 48).

1 Cut the tops off the fennel bulbs, and set aside 3 small bunches of fronds. Slice the bulbs into quarters, lengthwise through the core, but leaving some of the core attached to prevent the quarters from falling apart as they cook.

2 Put the fennel in a pan with enough cold water to cover, add 1 tsp salt and blanch over medium heat until tender, but not cooked through. Drain.

3 Melt the butter in a large pan over medium–high heat. Reduce heat to medium, add the fennel in a single layer and let brown for 2–3 minutes. Sprinkle with sugar and allow the sugar to caramelize, but not burn. Gently turn the fennel over to allow the other side to brown. The fennel should be tender, but still firm. Remove from heat and set aside.

4 Heat the olive oil in a pan until hot. Carefully add one bunch of fennel fronds at a time and quick-fry (about 20 seconds) each frond. Drain on a paper towel (kitchen paper) and keep covered until ready to use.

SERVES 6

3 large fennel bulbs, including fronds
4 tbsp/55g butter
1 tsp sugar
2 tbsp extra-virgin olive oil
sea salt

Sautéed Potatoes

Boiled, baked, or sautéed, potatoes and her youth on the farm go hand in hand for Debra Hall. She often serves them in one form or another, especially with a roast.

1 In a large pan bring the potatoes to a boil in salted water. Cook until the potatoes are almost tender, but still firm. Drain.

2 In a large skillet (frying pan), melt the butter over medium–high heat. Add potatoes, salt, and pepper and sauté until cooked. Add salt and pepper to taste.

SERVES 6

2 lb/900g mixed red and white small new potatoes

sea salt

3 tbsp/40g unsalted butter

ground black pepper

Tip

For a smoky flavor, put the roast pork (see page 48), cabbage, fennel, and potatoes in a cast iron skillet (frying pan) and heat over a wood-burning fire until hot, making sure the meat and vegetables do not burn. Remove from the heat and garnish with fried fennel fronds. Serve hot.

Savory Red Chard

2 bunches of red chard

2 tbsp extra-virgin olive oil

1 tbsp/15g butter

2–3 shallots (about ⅓ cup/55g), finely chopped

2 garlic cloves, finely chopped

1 tsp fresh thyme leaves

sea salt and ground black pepper

"I'd never tasted chard until the first year I found pre-started ruby red chard seedlings at a local nursery," says Barbara Jacksier. "I couldn't resist the shiny green leaves atop bright scarlet stems, so I bought quite a few and planted them in my garden." You won't be able to resist Barbara's quick-to-fix recipe.

1 Cut the ends of the stems off the chard and discard. Rinse the leaves and gather them together into 2 piles. Take each pile and roll it tightly. Cut them into thin strips crosswise.

2 Heat the oil and butter in a large, heavy skillet (frying pan) over medium heat. Sauté the shallots with the garlic, stirring often until lightly browned, about 3 minutes. Add the chard, salt and pepper to taste, and thyme. Cook, stirring often, for about 5 minutes or until the chard is tender but still retains its bright color. Serve hot.

Popovers

Braised beef brisket with gravy and popovers was a common Friday night dinner in Barbara Jacksier's mother's household. "My grandparents grew up in England and often served traditional Jewish dishes alongside British staples, reinterpreted in my grandmother's own unique way," she says. These luscious popovers are so good that they can be eaten on their own with a little pat of butter.

MAKES 6

butter, for greasing pan
2 eggs
1 cup/240ml milk
1 cup/115g unbleached all-purpose (plain) flour
1 tsp baking powder
½ tsp salt

1 Preheat the oven to 425°F/220°C/gas mark 7. Grease a six-cup popover (Yorkshire pudding) pan with butter, then place on a baking sheet in the oven until hot.

2 In a medium bowl, beat the eggs slightly, add milk and mix well. Beat in the flour, baking powder, and salt until just smooth, being careful not to overbeat.

3 Remove the hot pan from the oven and quickly fill the cups one-half full. Bake for 20 minutes, then decrease the oven temperature to 325°F/160°C/gas mark 3, and bake until the popover sides are firm and crusty, about 15–20 minutes.

4 Immediately remove from cups and serve piping hot.

Roasted Root Vegetables

Seasonal root vegetables are not only healthy but delicious as well. They can be served in numerous ways from soup, casseroles, or stews. But, roasting them brings forth their inimitable and distinctive flavors and make them the perfect sides for a roast, poultry, and fish. Serve these with the pot roast on page 76.

SERVES 6–8

1 rutabaga (swede)

1 large celery root (celeriac)

2 medium white turnips

2 parsnips

2 large yams (red sweet potatoes)

2 large Yukon Gold (Maris Piper) potatoes

6 baby artichokes, halved lengthwise

24 red and white pearl (pickling) onions, peeled and left whole

8 garlic cloves, peeled and left whole

4 tbsp chopped fresh herbs of choice (sage, thyme, rosemary)

olive oil

1 Peel and cube the rutabaga, celery root, turnips, parsnips, yams, and potatoes. Lightly oil a large baking sheet or pan.

2 Arrange the vegetables in the pan, adding the artichokes, onions, and garlic. Sprinkle with chopped herbs, then drizzle generously with olive oil. Toss the vegetables with your hands to coat them with the herbs and oil.

3 Add the pan of vegetables to the oven 20 minutes after you put in the pot roast (see page 76). Shake the pan or stir the vegetables occasionally. After 30 minutes check for doneness. Remove from the oven when the vegetables are tender.

Betty Botter bought some butter. "But," she said, "this butter's bitter.
If I put this bitter butter in my batter, it would make my batter bitter.
But a bit of better butter would make my bitter batter better."
So Betty Botter bought some butter, better than the bitter butter.
Made her bitter batter better.

(Old nursery rhyme)

chapter 4
desserts and baking

Ice Cream with Rhubarb-Bourbon Compote

As the saying goes, "the best laid plans of mice and men often go awry." And so it was when Anne Marie's oven broke down and she needed to substitute the dessert she had planned to serve for a farmhouse dinner party. A trip to the garden yielded plenty of rhubarb, that, with the help of a little bourbon and brown sugar, she cooked up into a rich and mellow topping for the sweet, creamy goodness of vanilla ice cream. It became an instant crowd-pleaser.

SERVES 6–8

12 rhubarb stalks, about
8 inches/20cm long

6 heaping tbsp/85g unsalted
butter

½ cup/115g dark brown sugar

¼ cup/60ml bourbon whiskey

vanilla ice cream, to serve

1 Cut rhubarb into ½-inch/1-cm pieces.

2 Melt 4 tbsp/55g butter in a skillet (frying pan) over low–medium heat. Add the rhubarb and sauté until it starts to become tender. Add the brown sugar. Cook, stirring gently, until the rhubarb is completely tender, making sure not to brown your sauce.

3 Melt the remaining butter in a pan over low heat, add the bourbon, and cook for about 4 minutes. Pour the bourbon sauce over the cooked rhubarb.

4 When ready to serve, put 2 scoops of vanilla ice cream in a bowl and top with 2 tbsp of the rhubarb–bourbon compote.

Mom's Dutch Apple Pie

With every bite of this delicious apple pie, Joy Waltmire fondly recalls the one her mom made for every church potluck and for special company. "It was always a favorite, especially in the fall when the McIntosh apples were in season, picked fresh," she reminisces. "It still is today." McIntosh apples are named for John McIntosh who discovered the first seedling in 1811. McIntosh apples grow particularly well in a cool climate and their aromatic flavor heralds the crisp days of fall.

1 Preheat the oven to 375°F/190°C/gas mark 5.

2 Prepare the pie crust according to the recipe instructions.

3 Make the filling: core, pare, and slice the apples. In a large bowl, toss the apples with the flour, sugar, and cinnamon. Arrange the apple mixture over the crust in a 10-inch/25cm pie plate.

4 Make the topping: in a bowl, mix the butter, brown sugar, flour, and chopped pecans together until crumbly. Spread over the apples.

5 Bake until bubbly and brown, about 40–45 minutes. Serve warm with vanilla ice cream.

SERVES 8

favorite pie crust recipe for single crust 10-inch/25cm pie

For the filling:
8–10 medium McIntosh (Granny Smith) apples, or favorite baking apples
¼ cup/4 tbsp flour
¼ cup/55g sugar
3 tbsp ground cinnamon

For the topping:
¾ stick/85g soft butter
¾ cup/170g dark brown sugar
½ cup/55g flour
¼–½ cup/25–55g chopped pecans, depending on your preference

vanilla ice cream, to serve

Wine-infused Blackberry Buttermilk Cake

SERVES 8–10

For the cake:

2 cups/225g cake flour (see Tips)

1 tsp baking powder

1 tsp baking soda (bicarbonate of soda)

¾ tsp sea salt

1 stick/115g unsalted butter

1 cup/240g organic evaporated cane juice

1 tsp vanilla extract (essence)

2 large eggs

1 cup/240ml buttermilk, well-shaken

For the topping:

¾ cup/180ml Sauternes (or any favorite dessert wine)

4 tbsp granulated sugar

1 heaping tbsp grated pink grapefruit zest

3 tbsp blackberry preserves (jam)

3–4 cups/450g fresh blackberries

buttermilk, to serve (optional)

freshly whipped cream, to serve (optional)

Angela Reed translated her memories of growing up with the sweet taste of wild blackberries into a no less-memorable dessert. Her blackberry buttermilk cake is a tribute to purple-stained fingers and lips, and scratches from the thorny brambles of the bushes. Buttermilk keeps this cake light, airy, and flavorful, and plump sun-ripened berries bring home summer's best.

1 Preheat the oven to 350°F/180°C/gas mark 4.

2 Line the bottom of a buttered 9 x 2-inch/23 x 5-cm round cake pan with a piece of wax paper (greaseproof paper) cut to fit. The easiest way to do this is to lay the pan on the wax paper and use a pencil or marker to trace it. Then cut out your shape a tiny bit inside the circle you drew. Butter the wax paper.

3 Sift together the flour, baking powder, baking soda, and salt.

4 Beat the butter and cane juice together in a large bowl with an electric mixer until pale and fluffy, then beat in the vanilla extract.

5 Add the eggs one at a time, beating well after each addition. With the mixer set on low speed, add the buttermilk until it just begins to combine with the butter, cane juice, and egg mixture (do not overmix). Add the flour mixture in three batches, mixing after each addition until gently combined (do not overmix).

6 Spoon the batter into the prepared pan, smoothing the top carefully. Set the pan on the middle rack of the oven, and bake until golden and a tester (a toothpick or a sharp knife) comes out clean, about 40–50 minutes. Cool in the pan on a wire rack. When cool, run a knife around the edge and slide the cake onto a serving plate. If the cake has bulged and will not lay flat. simply flip it over, bulge side up, and run a serrated knife gently, horizontally through the cake, thus cutting off the bump. This allows for much easier placement of the berries.

7 Make the topping. Bring the wine, 3 tbsp sugar, and the grapefruit zest to a boil in a small pan, stirring until the sugar is dissolved. Boil until the syrup is reduced to about ⅔ cup/140ml (1–2 minutes).

8 Reserve 2 tbsp syrup and pour the remainder slowly and evenly over the cake. Stir together the rest of the syrup, preserves, and remaining 1 tbsp sugar in a small pan, and simmer, stirring occasionally until thickened slightly, about 1 minute. It should be like thick syrup. Arrange the berries on the cake and pour the syrup over. Serve as warm as possible for the most "ooohs" and "aaahs" from your guests.

Tips

If cake flour is not available, substitute 1¾ cups/200g all-purpose (plain flour), plus 4 tbsp cornstarch (cornflour).

To fully savor the flavors of blackberry, grapefruit, and Sauternes, opt to eat this delightful cake "as is," but it is also delectable with a bit of buttermilk pooling around the cake, or topped with fresh whipped cream. If you are pressed for time, you can bake the cake one day ahead, wrapping it in plastic wrap (clingfilm) when fully cooled.

Raspberry Fields Berry Crumble

Located in the heart of the bucolic Hudson River Valley in upstate New York, Raspberry Fields Farm's heritage raspberries thrive with the help of a micro-flock of wooly weeding babydoll sheep and the hands-on care of the Higgins family. Sara Higgins proudly notes that "the homegrown berries are used in conjunction with our granola, made on site using old artisanal and organic methods by baking our products in small batches and without mechanization." Much like the farms of yesteryear, the Higgins family also partners with other local farms in sharing bounty and products.

1 Preheat the oven to 350°F/180°C/gas mark 4. Bake the granola until it becomes golden brown. Remove from the oven and set aside.

2 Place the raspberries in a microwave-safe bowl. Crumble the granola on top.

3 Microwave for approximately 2 minutes until the granola is soft and chewy, and the berries are warm.

4 To serve, top with yogurt or ice cream and top with fresh strawberries.

THIS RECIPE IS FOR INDIVIDUAL BOWLS OF BERRY CRUMBLE
To increase portions, fill ovenproof bowls with berries, top with granola and place on a baking sheet.

generous handful of granola of choice

a handful of raspberries, fresh or frozen

½ cup/115g yogurt or ice cream of choice, to serve

strawberries, to decorate

Dark Chocolate Chip Raspberry Cookies

Sara Higgins' cookies (baked in the "granolary" on the family Victorian-era farmette) blend bursts of rich dark chocolate and accents of flavorful raspberries, with chewy goodness made even better served with a hot cup of red raspberry herbal tea.

1 Preheat the oven to 375°F/190°C/gas mark 5.

2 Stir the flour, baking soda, salt, chocolate chips, and dried raspberries in a bowl. Set aside.

3 In a mixer, combine the canola oil, evaporated cane juice, brown sugar, and vanilla extract until smooth. Add the eggs one at a time. Add flour mixture a little at a time.

4 Using a 2 inch/5cm cookie scoop, place individual mounds of the mixture on parchment covered baking sheets and bake in batches if necessary, for 9–11 minutes until lightly brown.

5 Cool on the baking sheets before removing to wire racks.

MAKES 24

2¼ cups/250g unbleached all-purpose (plain) flour

1 tsp baking soda (bicarbonate of soda)

1 tsp sea salt

1½ cups/250g dark chocolate chips

1½ cups/250g whole dried raspberries

¾ cup/180ml canola (rapeseed) oil

¾ cup/170g evaporated cane juice, or white sugar

¾ cup/170g brown sugar

1 tsp vanilla extract (essence)

2 large free-range eggs

Rosemary Corn Muffins

Lulu Tapp admits that she is an herb lover, and she excels in incorporating their unique flavors in her recipes, as she demonstrates in pairing the aromatic intensity of rosemary with the cornmeal sweetness of her flavorful muffins.

MAKES 12 SMALL MUFFINS

1¼ cups/140g all-purpose (plain) flour
¾ cup/115g cornmeal (polenta)
¼ cup/50g sugar
2 tsp salt
½ cup/120ml skim milk (but any milk will work)
2 tsp fresh chopped rosemary
2 tsp fresh chopped thyme (optional)
¼ cup/60ml vegetable oil
1 egg, beaten

1 Preheat the oven to 400°F/200°C/gas mark 6.

2 Mix all the ingredients together in a large bowl.

3 Pour the batter evenly into nonstick muffin pans and bake for 15–20 minutes, or until a toothpick inserted in the center of the muffins comes out clean.

4 Remove from the oven and cool on a wire rack.

Blueberry Sour Cream Coffee Cake

Lizzie McGraw inherited her grandma's curiosity for experimenting with recipes. It is said that "the proof is in the pudding," but in this case, it is in Lizzie's favorite coffee cake flavored with pecans, dried cherries, and blueberries.

MAKES 12 INDIVIDUAL CAKES OR ONE 10 INCH/25CM ROUND CAKE

1 cup/225g unsalted butter, softened

2 cups/450g granulated sugar

4 eggs

2 tsp vanilla extract (essence)

3 cups/340g all-purpose (plain) flour

1 tsp baking soda (bicarbonate of soda)

1 tsp sea salt

2 cups/450g sour cream or Greek yogurt, or half sour cream and half yogurt

For the filling:

¾ cup/170g brown sugar

2 tbsp ground cinnamon

½ cup/50g walnuts or pecans

½ cup/85g raisins or dried cherries

1 cup/145g blueberries (if frozen, thaw and rinse well before using)

For the cream cheese icing:

¾ cup/170g cream cheese

⅓ cup/70g unsalted butter

1 tsp vanilla extract (essence)

2½–3 cups/280–340g sifted confectioners' (icing) sugar

¼ cup/60ml milk or water

lavender buds, to garnish

a few blueberries, to garnish

1 Preheat the oven to 350°F/180°C/gas mark 4.

2 In a large mixing bowl, cream the butter and sugar together until light and fluffy. Add the eggs one at a time and the vanilla extract, and whisk with an electric beater until well mixed. In another bowl, combine the flour, baking soda, and salt. Add the flour mixture and the sour cream to the wet mixture and beat until the batter is smooth.

3 In a small bowl, mix the sugar and cinnamon together. Set aside.

4 In a greased 10 inch/25cm bundt or tube pan, spoon in a 1 inch/2.5cm layer of batter. Sprinkle with one third of the cinnamon sugar mix, then add a layer of the walnuts, dried fruit, and blueberries. Repeat the layering process 2–3 times.

5 Bake for 60–65 minutes, or until a toothpick inserted in the center comes out clean. If using mini bundt pans, reduce the baking time to 35–40 minutes and test for doneness.

6 Remove from the oven, transfer to a wire rack, and cool for 20–30 minutes before removing from the pan.

7 Make the icing. Beat all the ingredients together to make a smooth icing.

8 When completely cool, frost with the cream cheese icing, or for a lighter topping, simply dust the top of the cake with confectioners' (icing) sugar. Garnish either with a few sprinkles of lavender buds or blueberries.

Lavender Blueberry Pancakes

Many of the dishes she loves to make are variations of recipes Lizzie McGraw inherited from beloved relatives. Lizzie brings her own touch to familiar pancakes by adding edible lavender buds, that elevate a simple recipe to a culinary delight.

1 In a bowl, mix all the ingredients except the lavender and blueberries until well blended. The batter does not need to be super smooth.

2 Place about three quarters of the lavender buds in a pan, cover with water and bring to a boil. Blanch for 1 minute. Drain, and add the blanched lavender to the batter. Mix gently. Add three quarters of the blueberries. Mix again.

3 Pour ¼ cup/60ml batter in a hot skillet (frying pan). When the batter bubbles, turn the pancake over and keep cooking until golden. Set the cooked pancake aside.

4 Repeat until all the batter is used. Stack the finished pancakes on a plate and garnish with the remaining lavender and blueberries.

MAKES ABOUT 12–15 PANCAKES, SERVES 4

1 cup/240ml buttermilk
2 large eggs
½ tsp salt
1 tsp vanilla extract (essence)
1 tsp baking powder
1 cup/115g all-purpose (plain) flour
1 cup/45g edible lavender buds
1 cup/145g fresh blueberries

Lemon-glazed Cupcakes

MAKES 12 CUPCAKES

For the cupcakes:

1½ cups/170g all-purpose (plain) flour

2 tsp baking powder

½ tsp salt

½ cup/120ml buttermilk

1 tsp vanilla extract (essence)

juice and zest of 1 lemon

½ cup/115g unsalted butter, softened

1 cup/225g granulated sugar

2 eggs

For the lemon cream cheese topping:

1 cup/225g cream cheese, softened

½ stick/55g unsalted butter, softened

1¾ cups/225g confectioners' icing) sugar

1 tsp vanilla extract (essence)

¼ tsp grated lemon zest

juice of 1 lemon

Erin Shepherd's cupcakes' subtle flavor and rich, moist goodness come from the delicate infusion of lemon juice and alternatively mixing in the wet and dry ingredients (don't be tempted to skip that step, it really makes a difference). Light and lovely, these sweet treats are a feast for the taste buds and perfect for a tea party.

1 Preheat the oven to 350°F/180°C/gas mark 4. Prepare the cupcake pans by spraying them with nonstick cooking spray or by using paper liners.

2 Combine the flour, baking powder, and salt in a bowl. Set aside.

3 In another bowl, whisk together the buttermilk, vanilla extract, lemon zest, and juice. Set aside.

4 In the bowl of an electric mixer, cream the butter and sugar together. Add the eggs, one at a time, and beat well. With the mixer on low, add the flour mixture alternately with the buttermilk mixture, beginning and ending with the flour.

5 Fill the pans about three-quarters full. Bake until a toothpick inserted in the center of a cupcake comes out clean, about 20 minutes.

6 Cool for 10 minutes in the pan, then remove to a wire rack.

7 To make the lemon cream cheese topping, with a mixer, blend the butter and cream cheese together until well combined. Slowly add in the confectioners' sugar until fully blended. Add the vanilla extract, lemon zest, and juice.

8 Spread a thin layer of the lemon cream cheese topping over each cupcake.

Blueberry Muffins

Berrybogg Farm, in Strafford, New Hampshire, has been run by the Lake family since Nate and Anne Lake began planting the 6,000 highbush blueberry plants over 30 years ago. Today, their daughter Julie and her husband Michael help Anne run the farm, and keep the long-standing family tradition flourishing. Throughout August, weekends see many of the same customers return year after year for the chance to harvest blueberries with their families, and enjoy luscious pies, muffins, jams, and jellies from the farm stand, and a peaceful day in the country. Berrybogg Farm blueberries can get quite large, so Julie suggests using larger muffin tins to accommodate the plump berries, and not overwhelm the muffin texture.

1 Preheat the oven to 375°F/190°C/gas mark 5.

2 Combine the sugar and oil. In a separate bowl, beat the egg and milk together. Sift the dry ingredients together and add alternately with the milk and egg mixture to the sugar mixture. Fold in the blueberries.

3 Pour into greased muffin pans. Combine the sugar and cinnamon and sprinkle mixture on top of each muffin. Bake for 25–30 minutes.

MAKES 6 EXTRA-LARGE OR 12 REGULAR SIZE MUFFINS

½ cup/115g granulated sugar

⅓ cup/75ml canola (rapeseed) oil

1 egg

½ cup/120ml milk

1½ cups/170g all-purpose (plain) flour

2 tsp baking powder

¼ tsp baking soda (bicarbonate of soda)

½ tsp salt

1 cup/145g blueberries

2 tbsp sugar

2 tsp ground cinnamon

Strawberry Delight

Tracey Leber knows that the inimitable flavor of juicy, ripe strawberries, rich finely-textured pound cake, and fresh whipped cream are made for each other. Throughout the summer, Tracey serves this traditional dessert to gatherings of friends on balmy afternoons or as a fitting ending to a family meal.

1 Preheat the oven to 350°F/180°C/gas mark 4. Prepare two 2lb/900g loaf pans with butter and flour.

2 Sift the flour and baking powder together and set aside.

3 In a large mixing bowl, cream the butter, sugar, and vanilla seeds. Mix in the eggs, and beat on high for 5 minutes. Reduce the speed to low and alternately add the flour mixture and milk, beating well each time. Spoon the batter into the pans and smooth flat.

4 Bake for 75 minutes, checking after 60 minutes. If the cakes are browning too much, drape them loosely with foil. Allow to cool for 15 minutes before removing from the pan.

5 Toss the strawberries with the sugar and place in a bowl. Let sit until the juices have pooled around the strawberries or prepare ahead of time, and store in the refrigerator.

6 Whip the cream: in a large stand mixer, add the cream and whisk on low for 2 minutes. As the cream begins to thicken, add the sugar, and increase the speed to high. The cream is ready when it begins to form peaks.

7 Assemble the individual desserts with one thick slice of pound cake, a dollop of whipped cream, and strawberries on top.

MAKES 2 LOAVES OF CAKE

For the pound cake:

3 cups/340g all-purpose (plain) flour

1 tsp baking powder

2 sticks/225g butter, at room temperature

2 cups/450g sugar

1½ vanilla beans (pods), seeds scraped

5 eggs 1 cup/240ml milk

butter and flour, for loaf pans

For the strawberries:

1 lb/450g fresh strawberries, hulled and sliced

1 tbsp sugar

For the whipped cream:

1 pint/480ml heavy (double) cream

3 tbsp confectioners' (icing) sugar

Strawberry-Almond Tart

9-inch/23cm store-bought pie crust or
favorite homemade tart shell recipe

For the filling:

1 stick/115g unsalted butter, at room
temperature

8 oz /225g almond paste, cut into
1 inch/2.5cm cubes

¼ cup/50g sugar

1 tsp grated lemon zest

1 tsp fresh lemon juice

1 tsp vanilla extract (essence)

¾ tsp almond extract (essence)

2 eggs

⅓ cup/5 tbsp unbleached all-purpose
(plain) flour

For the topping:

2 tsp unsalted butter

1½ cups/170g slivered (flaked) blanched
almonds

½ cup/140g strawberry preserves (jam)

I owe everything I know about food to my mother, including my never-ending lust for desserts. My mom was an excellent cook and a pastry maven. I can still clearly see the tantalizing pies, tarts, and other pastries she baked for my sister and I. She always used seasonal ingredients at their seasonal peak for freshness and flavor. Her luscious treats were as irresistible to the eye as they were to the taste buds. In our home, no meal was complete without dessert, like this ambrosial tart. Every time I make it, it fills me with visions of maternal love and the comforts of home.

1 If making your own tart shell, prepare the pastry according to the recipe instructions and carefully transfer to a 9-inch/23cm tart pan. Refrigerate until firm, about 30 minutes.

2 Preheat the oven to 375°F/190°C/gas mark 5.

3 Line the pastry shell with parchment paper or aluminum foil and fill with dried beans. Bake for 10 minutes, remove the paper and beans and bake another 5–10 minutes, or until the shell is pale golden. Remove from the oven and transfer to a wire rack. Reduce oven temperature to 350°F/180°C/gas mark 4.

4 Make the filling: using an electric mixer on medium speed, or a whisk, beat the butter until smooth. Add the almond paste, one piece at a time, beating until smooth.

5 Continuing beating while gently adding the sugar, lemon zest, lemon juice, vanilla extract, and almond extract. Add the eggs one at a time, beating well after each addition. Stir in the flour.

6 Make the topping: melt 2 tsp butter in a skillet (frying pan) over low heat. Add the silvered almonds, stirring gently until golden (being careful not to burn the almonds). Remove from the heat and let cool.

7 Assemble the tart: spread the almond paste mixture evenly in the partially baked tart shell. Return the tart to the oven and bake for 35–45 minutes, or until the center of the filling is firm to the touch. Remove from the oven and let cool on a wire rack.

8 Spread the strawberry preserves evenly over the top of the tart. Arrange the toasted almonds in a circular pattern on top of the tart, making sure to let some of the strawberry preserves show in the center. Serve at room temperature.

Lemon Sour Cream Pie

This tempting recipe is one of the many passed to Maria Carr by her mom, Trudy Farrier. Bursting with fresh lemon juice and topped with billows of whipped cream, this scrumptious pie is the perfect balance of tartness and sweetness.

MAKES 1 SINGLE CRUST PIE

For the pie crust:

2 cups/225g all-purpose (plain) flour

1¼ tsp salt

2 sticks/225g cold butter

½ cup/120ml cold water

For the filling:

1¼ cups/280g granulated sugar

⅓ cup/ 5 tbsp cornstarch (cornflour)

2 eggs

½ cup/120ml fresh lemon juice

1½ cups/360ml boiling water

½ cup/115g sour cream

1 tbsp/15g butter

For the topping:

1 pint/480ml heavy (double) cream

1 tsp vanilla extract (essence)

2 tbsp granulated sugar

½ cup/75g blueberries

1 Make the pie crust. Sift the flour and salt together. Cut the cold butter into the flour until the mixture resembles cornmeal. Add cold water by gently stirring it into the flour and butter mixture until completely moistened (do not over stir).

2 Divide the dough in half and refrigerate for at least 2 hours. Freeze half the dough for another time.

3 Roll the pie dough out to 12 inches/30cm in diameter and ⅛-inch/3mm thick. Press the pie dough firmly into a 10-inch/25-cm pie pan. Pinch off any excess dough around the edges. Put in the freezer for 30 minutes.

4 Preheat the oven to 400°F/200°C/gas mark 6.

5 Line the pie crust with a sheet of heavy aluminum foil. Fill with dried beans, uncooked rice, or metal weights (this will help prevent the pie shell from shrinking while baking). Bake the lined crust until it dries out, about 15 minutes (the crust will be ready once the aluminum foil can easily be removed).

6 Reduce the oven temperature to 350°F/180°C/gas mark 4. Remove the foil and weights and return pie crust to the oven. Bake for another 10 minutes, or until the crust is golden brown.

7 Make the filling. Combine and mix well the sugar, cornstarch, and eggs over medium heat. Gradually stir in the lemon juice and boiling water.

8 Cook and stir the mixture over medium heat until it comes to a boil and thickens. Let boil for one minute. Remove from the heat.

9 Fold in the sour cream and butter. Refrigerate for 3 hours. Fill the crust with chilled custard.

10 To make the topping, whisk the cream on high speed with an electric mixer for about 3 minutes. Add the vanilla extract and the sugar. Beat for one more minute.

11 Gently spoon the whipped cream over the custard. Top with the blueberries. Keep refrigerated until ready to serve.

Sour Cherry Tart

This is actually a cake, but Barbara Jacksier's grandmother called any small cake that had fruit in it a tart! "The basic cream cake recipe is my mother's, but the addition of sour cherries is mine."One year when I had a bumper crop of sour cherries, I threw a few cups into the mix and everyone loved it," Barbara says. "This cake is equally delicious if you use peaches, plums, pears, or apples, instead of cherries."

1 Preheat the oven to 375°F/190°C/gas mark 5.

2 Grease the bottom of an 8 inch/20cm round baking pan with softened butter.

3 In a mixing bowl, beat the eggs with an electric mixer until foamy and light yellow. Mix in the sugar and the cream and set aside.

4 In a separate bowl, use a wooden spoon to mix the flour with the baking powder and cinnamon.

5 Add the flour mixture to the egg mixture and mix until well blended. Stir in the cherries. Pour the batter into the prepared pan and bake for 40–50 minutes or until done.

SERVES 6–8

butter, for greasing pan

3 eggs

1 cup/225g granulated sugar

1 cup/240ml heavy (double) cream

1½ cups/170g all-purpose (plain) flour

2 tsp baking powder

½ tsp ground cinnamon

2 cups/340g sour cherries, pitted

Hearty Apple Crisp

One of Erin Shepherd's go-to desserts is her apple crisp. "This crisp gives you all the flavor of an apple pie, but is quicker to make," she says. "Apple crisps can be dry but this one isn't! The secret is the inclusion of applesauce."

1 Preheat the oven to 350°F/180°C/gas mark 4.

2 In a large bowl, stir together the apples, applesauce, butter, brown sugar, and spices until combined and the apples are well coated.

3 In a separate bowl, stir together the melted butter, oats, sugar, flour, and cinnamon. Spoon the apple filling into a baking dish or individual ramekins, and top with the oat mixture.

4 Bake for approximately 25–30 minutes or until golden brown.

5 Serve warm with a dollop of fresh whipped cream or ice cream.

MAKES ONE 8–9 INCH/20–23CM CRISP OR 8 ONE-CUP INDIVIDUAL CRISPS

For the filling:

1¼ lb/560g apples of various varieties, sliced and peeled (diced if making individual crisps)

1–1½ cups/450g unsweetened or homemade applesauce

4 tbsp/55g cold butter, cut into small cubes

2 tbsp brown sugar

1 tsp ground cinnamon

1 tsp ground allspice

1 tsp ground coriander

½ tsp grated nutmeg

For the oat topping:

1 stick/115g butter, melted

1 cup/100g old-fashioned rolled (porridge) oats

½ cup/115g brown sugar

½ cup/55g whole wheat flour

½ tsp ground cinnamon

fresh whipped cream or vanilla ice cream

Strawberry-Raspberry Tart with Rosemary Whipped Cream

SERVES 6–8

For the tart crust:

¾ cup/85g organic all-purpose (plain) flour

½ cup/50g organic whole wheat (wholemeal) flour

¾ stick/85g cold, unsalted butter, cut into small pieces

3 tbsp mild olive oil

¼ tsp salt

¼ cup/50g sugar

1–2 tbsp ice water

1 egg white

1–2 tsp water

For the filling:

4 tbsp dark brown sugar

1 lb/450g fresh organic strawberries, sliced

1 pint/130g organic raspberries

2 tbsp/25g unsalted butter, cut into small pieces

For the rosemary simple syrup:

4-inch/10cm sprig fresh rosemary

½ cup/120ml water

½ cup/115g sugar

For the rosemary whipped cream:

1 pint/480ml heavy (double) cream

½ cup/115g sugar

¼ cup/60ml rosemary simple syrup

Jennifer Rizzo's charming dessert is a big hit with her family. She favors this freeform galette over traditional tarts for its easy preparation, crisp crust, and versatility. Throughout spring and summer, Jennifer prefers a filling of raspberries and strawberries, but many other fresh fruits will work as well. From juicy cherries, fragrant pears, and crunchy apples, the many possibilities make this deceptively simple dessert perfect for any season. Spoonfuls of rosemary-infused fresh whipped cream complement both this tart's taste and texture.

1 First make the crust. In a large bowl, mix the flours, butter, olive oil, salt, and sugar with a pastry cutter or knives until the mixture is coarse. Add enough ice water to moisten the dough so that it holds together, but is not sticky. Knead the dough slightly to form into a ball. Wrap in wax paper (greaseproof paper) and chill in the refrigerator for 1 hour, or until ready to use.

2 Remove the dough from the refrigerator and press into a round on a baking sheet until the dough is approximately 12 inches/30cm round and ⅛ inch/3mm thick, pushing the edges up to make a small wall to hold in the juices.

3 In a small bowl, whisk the egg white with the water to make an egg wash. With a pastry brush, gently "paint' the edge of the tart. The crust is now ready to fill.

4 Preheat the oven to 375°F/190°C/gas mark 5.

5 Sprinkle the crust with half the brown sugar. Layer the strawberries in the crust in a circular pattern. Layer the raspberries on top, filling any gaps. Sprinkle with the remaining brown sugar and dot the top of the tart with the butter.

6 Bake the tart for 35–45 minutes (ovens vary, so check during the last 10 minutes to make sure it does not burn). Remove from the oven when the crust is lightly browned, and the fruit is just beginning to caramelize.

7 Make the simple syrup. In a small saucepan, bring the rosemary, water, and sugar to a boil, stirring. Let boil for approximately 2 minutes until all of the sugar is dissolved. Remove from the heat. Let the rosemary steep in the syrup until cool. Remove the rosemary sprig, separate the leaves from the stem, and finely chop the leaves until they are tiny speck-size pieces. Set aside.

8 Make the whipped cream. In a mixing bowl, place the sugar, simple syrup, chopped rosemary, and cream. Taste before whipping for sweetness and flavor. Mix with an electric beater on high until the mixture starts to get foamy, then thick. Watch carefully, and check every minute or so to see if it will hold a peak when you pull up the beaters. If it does, it's done. If you overbeat it, you'll end up with some tasty rosemary butter!

9 Serve the tart at room temperature topped with a generous dollop of rosemary whipped cream.

Tips

Any fresh fruit will work in the tart. Try peaches and blueberries for a flavorful alternative.

Rosemary simple syrup can be made in large batches by increasing ingredients equally and can also be used in lemonade, iced tea, brushed over sponge cake, or drizzled over ice cream. It will keep for up to two weeks in the refrigerator.

Any edible herbs can be used to make the simple syrup. Basil, mint, or even lavender offer delicious alternatives.

The rosemary simple syrup can be replaced with blended strawberries or raspberries in the whipped cream.

Maple Muffins

MAKES 12 MUFFINS

2 cups/225g whole wheat (wholemeal) flour

½ cup packed/115g brown sugar

2 tsp baking powder

1 tsp ground cinnamon

½ tsp salt

4 tbsp/55g unsalted butter

2 eggs, beaten

½ cup/120ml milk

1 tsp honey

1 tbsp grated orange zest

½ cup/120ml maple syrup

¼ cup/60ml maple syrup for drizzling (optional)

Elizabeth Mears became a fan of maple syrup when she moved from England to a farmhouse in the heart of Vermont a few years ago. The sweet golden syrup—made from the sap of the sugar maple tree—imparts an authentic and unparalleled flavor to the muffins that have become Elizabeth's children's favorite after-school treat.

1 Preheat the oven to 375°F/190°C/gas mark 5. Grease the cups of a 12-cup muffin pan.

2 Sift together the flour, sugar, baking powder, cinnamon, and salt. Cut in the butter until the mixture resembles coarse crumbs. Add the eggs, milk, honey, orange zest, and ½ cup/120ml maple syrup. Stir until all the ingredients are moistened. Fill the greased muffin tins three-quarters full.

3 Bake for 20–25 minutes, or until a toothpick inserted in the center of a muffin comes out clean. Remove from the oven and transfer to a wire rack. Let cool somewhat before taking the muffins out of the pan.

4 Drizzle maple syrup over the muffins if you like. Serve warm.

Banana Bread

Tracey Leber inherited her banana bread recipe from her grandmother. Though the recipe is simple, the delectable results make this cake-like bread's sweet flavor and moist texture as enjoyable with a morning cup of coffee, an after-school snack, or as a dessert.

1 Preheat the oven to 350°F/180°C/gas mark 4. Butter a 2lb/900g loaf pan and set aside.

2 In a large bowl, mash the bananas and combine with the butter, eggs, and milk. Mix in the sugar, cinnamon, baking soda, baking powder, and salt. Slowly add the flour until combined.

3 Bake for 70 minutes, or until a toothpick inserted in the center of the loaf comes out clean. Cool before removing from the pan.

MAKES 1 LOAF

4 medium bananas, very ripe

4 tbsp/50g butter, at room temperature

2 eggs

2 tbsp milk

1 cup/225g granulated sugar

1 tsp ground cinnamon

1¼ tsp baking soda (bicarbonate of soda)

½ tsp baking powder

1 tsp salt

2 cups/225g all-purpose (plain) flour

Bread Pudding

SERVES 6–8

4 cups/150g stale cubed bread (most bread will work; croissants, brioches, and Italian panettone are also excellent)

2 cups/480ml heavy (double) cream

4 tbsp/55g melted butter

2 tsp vanilla extract (essence)

¼ cup/60ml rum

1 tsp ground cinnamon

¼ cup/50g brown sugar

½ cup/85g raisins or other dried fruit (optional)

4 eggs, beaten

Since its humble beginnings—created by frugal cooks who did not want to waste stale bread—this lowly pudding has evolved from a basic baked bread and milk mixture into a quintessential winter treat. In the Beall household, this wholesome dessert is comfort food at its best, regardless of the season.

1 Preheat the oven to 350°F/180°C/gas mark 4.

2 Place the cubed bread in a large bowl.

3 In a large pan, blend together the cream, butter, vanilla extract, rum, cinnamon, sugar, and raisins, and heat until simmering. Stir until the sugar is fully dissolved. Remove from the heat. Add the beaten eggs and stir well.

4 Slowly pour the egg mixture over the bread, allowing the bread to soak up the mixture, then pour the bread pudding into a buttered 1½-quart/1½-liter baking dish.

5 Bake for 45 minutes until the top of the bread pudding forms a golden crust. Serve hot.

Herb French Bread

There is nothing quite as delicious as the scent of baking bread, and Joy Waltmire's is no exception. Olive oil and an infusion of herbs give it its amazing fragrance and savory quality, and cornmeal its rustic crust. Big chunks of this old-fashioned bread are meant to be dunked in steamy winter soups and stews, or enjoyed as a great snack with cheese.

1 Chop the basil, thyme, marjoram, oregano (and sage if desired) very finely. Set aside.

2 Proof two packs of yeast in 1 tbsp water with the sugar. When bubbly and doubled in volume, add to the flour and sea salt. Stir in the chopped herbs.

3 Mix together the warm water, egg, and olive oil. Add to the flour mixture and mix thoroughly until the dough is not sticky, adding more flour if necessary.

4 Set aside in a warm place and let dough rise until doubled.

5 Preheat the oven to 400°F/200°C/gas mark 6.

6 Form the dough into a rustic, not perfect loaf. Place in a French bread pan (approximately 16 inches/40cm long), greased with olive oil and coated with cornmeal.

7 Bake for 20–25 minutes, until golden. Serve warm.

MAKES 1 LOAF

1 tbsp each fresh basil, thyme, marjoram, oregano, sage (optional)

2¼ oz/7g packs instant (fast action) dry yeast

1 tbsp warm water

1 tbsp sugar

3 cups/340g unbleached all-purpose (plain) flour

1 tsp sea salt

1 cup/240ml warm water

1 egg

⅓ cup/75ml extra-virgin olive oil, plus extra for bread pan

1 tbsp cornmeal (polenta)

Farmhouse Bread

Monica Savage, one of Maria Carr's ten siblings, shares her recipe for this crusty, dense loaf.

1 Mix the yeast, salt, and sugar together in a bowl. Add the warm water to the yeast mixture. Stir with a wire whisk and let sit for 10 minutes, until frothy.

2 Stir the yeast mixture with a whisk again. Add both flours 1 cup/115g at a time, stirring with a whisk until all 6 cups of flour are thoroughly incorporated.

3 Knead the dough for 8 minutes (this can either be done by hand or with a dough hook attached to an electric mixer).

4 Cover the dough with a warm, damp dish towel and let rise for 1 hour. During this rising process, stir the dough down with a spoon every 10 minutes, a total of six times.

5 Preheat the oven to 400°F/200°C/gas mark 6. Spray cooking oil onto a baking sheet.

6 Divide the dough into two halves. Form into two loaves and let rise on the baking sheet for 20 minutes before putting them into the oven.

7 Bake for approximately 20–25 minutes. When the bottom of the loaves are golden brown, the loaves are ready. Remove from the oven and cool on a wire rack.

MAKES 2 LOAVES

2 tbsp instant (fast action) dry yeast

1 tbsp sea salt

2 tbsp granulated sugar

3 cups/720ml warm water

3 cups/350g unbleached all-purpose (plain) flour

3 cups/350g unbleached whole wheat (wholemeal) flour

Cracked Wheat Bread

Hot-from-the-oven thick slices of Tracey Leber's cracked wheat bread, lathered with her homemade chive butter (see opposite), are as much a treat on their own as they are with any meal or for ham, egg, or cheese sandwiches.

Place the water and honey in the pan of a bread machine and layer the dry ingredients on top, ending with the yeast. Follow bread machine setting for basic bread.

MAKES 1 LOAF

This recipe is for use with a bread machine.

1¼ cups/300ml warm water

2 tbsp honey

2 tbsp/25g butter at room temperature

2 tbsp dry milk powder

1¾ tsp salt

2 cups/225g strong bread flour

1⅓ cup/150g whole wheat (wholemeal) flour

¼ cup/40g cracked wheat

1¼ tsp instant (fast action) dry yeast

Old-fashioned Chive Butter

1 Pour the cream into the canning jar. Place lid on and shake vigorously. As the butter begins to form it will start to separate and liquid (buttermilk) will appear.

2 Once the clump of butter is formed, carefully pour out all of the "buttermilk." Add a bit of cold water to the canning jar, and shake again to be sure that all of the "buttermilk" has been removed from the butter. Pour out the water and repeat the process until the water comes out clean.

3 Transfer the butter onto the cheesecloth set over a container to drain any extra liquid, and refrigerate. Once the butter begins to solidify, fold in the chives and season with salt to taste. Serve cold or at room temperature.

MAKES ABOUT ½ CUP/115G BUTTER

1 cup/240ml heavy (double) cream
3 tbsp fresh chives, chopped
sea salt, to taste (optional)
1 pint/500ml canning jar with tight fitting lid
cheesecloth (muslin)

And the Quangle Wangle said
to himself on the crumpety tree
"Jam and jelly and bread
are the best food for me."

Edward Lear

chapter 5
drinks and preserves

Old-fashioned Lemonade

Lemons from a local grove, mint from her garden, and a simple syrup make Lulu Tapp's lemonade taste just like the one her grandma used to serve. For Lulu, the drink's sweet, refreshing flavor is forever associated with her childhood summer vacations spent climbing lemon trees in her grandmother's garden, and squeezing the juice from the fruit to help her grandma make pitchers-full of the delicious concoction.

1 Bring 1 quart/1 liter water to a boil. Add the sugar, lemon juice, and 6 mint leaves. Stir well. Remove from heat and let cool.

2 Pour into a 1-gallon/4-liter pitcher (jug). Add the remaining water, 6 mint leaves, and lemon slices, reserving one slice for each glass. Add the ice. Stir well.

3 Pour into tall glasses and garnish each drink with a mint sprig and slice of lemon.

MAKES ABOUT 1 GALLON/ 4 LITERS OR 12 x 8-OZ/240ML SERVINGS

3 quarts/3 liters water
2 cups/ 450g granulated sugar
juice of 12 large lemons
4 medium lemons, sliced
12 fresh mint leaves
2 cups/500ml ice cubes
fresh mint sprigs, to garnish

Preserved Lemons

Long before it became a cookery staple, lemon pickle and its use in sauces for fish meat and poultry was a way of life for Native Americans. The method was also featured in "A New System of Domestic Cooking" by Maria Eliza Rundell, written in 1808. In summer, the branches of Susie Beall's lemon trees are heavy with their fruits' ripe golden orbs. That's when Susie picks them to capture their radiance and fragrance to preserve and use to infuse main courses, salads, and sauces, just like it was done centuries ago.

1 Put 1 inch/2.5cm salt into the bottom of the jar.

2 Cut the lemons into vertical quarters, but not all the way through. Open the lemons and coat the insides with salt. Press to close back into a lemon shape and place in the jar. Repeat until you have one layer of lemons. Fill the jar with lemon juice to cover the lemons. Repeat until the jar is full.

3 Add peppercorns, thyme, and bay leaves. Cover and refrigerate for at least one month before using.

1-quart/1-liter canning jar
6–8 lemons
2 cups/450g kosher salt or coarse sea salt
2 cups/480ml fresh lemon juice
black peppercorns
fresh thyme sprigs
4 bay leaves

Tips

The liquid for preserving the lemons is great used in marinades and salad dressings. It can also be brushed over a chicken before grilling or braising it.

Preserved lemons can be used to make lemon butter by chopping them finely and mixing them with butter and herbs.

A tablespoon of finely chopped preserved lemon rind, mixed with ¼ stick/25g butter and 2 tbsp olive oil is a superb coating for two 8 oz/225g salmon fillets to be broiled/grilled.

Lemon Vinaigrette

½ preserved lemon, chopped
1 cup/240ml extra-virgin olive oil
¼ cup/60ml dry white wine
½ tsp ground black pepper
¼ tsp ground cumin

Combine all the ingredients in a food processor until well-blended. Use as a dressing for salads. It is especially good with avocados.

Honey Grape Lemonade

On a hot summer day, this quick, easy, and refreshing old-fashioned crowd pleaser made with just a few ingredients is all you need to chill out, and the kids will thank you!

SERVES 10

1 quart/1 liter white grape juice
juice of 5 large lemons
2½ cups/600ml water
honey, to taste
12 small ice cubes
2 lemons, thinly sliced

In a large pitcher, mix together the grape juice, lemon juice, and water. Stir well. Add honey to sweeten, to taste. Add ice cubes. Chill for 1 hour before serving. Float with lemon slices.

Strawberry-Rhubarb Honey Jam

MAKES 4 9-OZ/250G JARS

3 cups/450g rhubarb, chopped
into ½–1-inch/1–2.5-cm pieces

½ cup/120ml water

3 cups/675g fresh strawberries,
mashed

2 tbsp fresh lemon juice

1¼ cups/420g honey

2 x 1.75 oz/50g packs pectin

In late spring, Berrybogg Farm's blueberries begin to blossom and Julie Butterfield's bumblebees are busy pollinating the early varieties. Julie favors bumblebees over honeybees for their ability to pollinate blueberry flowers, and to tolerate cooler temperatures, wind, and even light rain. But, when the conditions are right, honeybees join in to maximize pollination, and the creation of the golden honey. The honey's natural sweetness tempers the tartness of the rhubarb and strawberry jam Julie makes in the traditional manner she learned from her mother, Anne Lake.

When making jams with honey, keep in mind that honey can have many different flavors depending on where it is from, and which flowers were used by the bees to obtain the nectar. To prevent the honey from overpowering the taste of the fruit, go light on the amount based on the type of honey you use. The more potent the honey, the less you will need. Rhubarb, which is actually a vegetable, is very tart on its own and needs the addition of some kind of sweetener (honey or sugar) to temper the tartness. This particular recipe has a loose consistency, but could be made firmer with the addition of more powdered pectin.

1 Sterilize the jars. Boil the lids for 5 minutes to soften sealing compound. Keep jars and lids hot until ready to use.

2 In a non-reactive pan, combine the rhubarb and water. Bring to a boil, then reduce heat, and simmer until the rhubarb is tender. Add the strawberries and lemon juice. Simmer until the mixture is soft (about 5–10 minutes).

3 Add the honey and bring to a boil stirring constantly. Add the pectin and boil hard for 1 minute, stirring constantly. Remove from the heat, and skim off foam, if necessary.

4 Ladle the hot jam into the jars and leave ¼ inch/5mm at the top for headspace.

5 Wipe jar rim if necessary and cover with the lids. Place jars in boiling water bath for 10 minutes. Store in a cool, dark place.

Spiced Pomegranate-Apple Cider

There is nothing quite as satisfying as hot cider, especially on a nippy afternoon. Caroline Verschoor's familiar fall drink gets a fruity flair with pomegranate juice and orange rind. Cloves spice up the natural sweetness of the honey, maple syrup, vanilla bean, and star anise. Delicious and comforting, this drink is equally loved by kids and adults. You can be sure they will ask for more so make extra batches. Just reheat them as needed.

1 In a large pan combine the cider, pomegranate juice, and maple syrup.

2 Add the cinnamon sticks, cloves, vanilla bean, star anise, and orange zest. Bring mixture to a boil; reduce heat. Cover and simmer for 15 minutes. Strain to remove all solids.

3 Serve warm, garnished with clove-studded orange slices if desired.

MAKES ABOUT 16 SERVINGS

1 gallon/3.8 liters pasteurized apple cider
1 pint/480ml pomegranate juice
4 tbsp maple syrup
2 cinnamon sticks
6 whole cloves
½ vanilla bean (pod)
3 star anise
4 oranges, peeled, zest reserved

For the garnish:
2 oranges, thinly sliced, studded with cloves, and cut into crescents (optional)

Tip
You can either discard the four oranges that are needed for the zest, or juice them and add the juice to the apple cider and pomegranate juice.

Chunky Applesauce with Cranberries and Fresh Mint

Barbara Jacksier's Virginia property came with several mature apple trees, and homemade applesauce became a regular addition to her dessert repertoire. On Thanksgiving, in order to make the dessert seem more special, she cubes the raw apples and cooks them until fork tender and adds cranberry for an unexpected touch of color and flavor.

SERVES 6–8

4–6 lb/1.8–2.7kg of crisp apples
ground cinnamon, to taste
granulated sugar, to taste (optional)
½ cup/55g fresh cranberries, lightly steamed
fresh mint leaves

1 Peel and core the apples and cut into small cubes. Put into a heavy pan with ½ inch/1cm water. Cook over medium heat, stirring frequently.

2 When the apples start to soften, add cinnamon to taste. If the apples need sweetening, add sugar, a tablespoon at a time.

3 Remove from heat when the apples are soft but still retain their shape. Cover and let stand for one hour before refrigerating until ready to serve.

4 To serve, top the applesauce with cranberries and snippets of mint. Garnish with a sprig of fresh mint.

Herb-infused Oils and Vinegars

Infusing oils and vinegars with fresh herbs keeps summer goodness at hand year-round and is one of Barbara Jacksier's favorite ways to add zing and zest to salads and vegetables. These easy concoctions also make great hostess gifts.

By choosing and mixing oils that are pale (canola [rapeseed], safflower, or sunflower) or yellow and green (corn or olive oils), you can create a rainbow of flavorful oils with single and mixed herb blends. Always wash bottles in very hot water and dry thoroughly before using (for added safety, run bottles through the dishwasher cycle before using). The amount of oil needed will vary for each blend based on the size of the bottle. The amount of herbs can be increased to suit personal tastes.

Tuck a few sprigs of herbs into a bottle, fill with the vinegar of your choice and let age. Sprinkle on salads and cooked vegetables for "just-picked" flavor. Nothing could be easier!

Basil Oil

2 cups/30g fresh sweet basil leaves

olive oil

1 sprig of basil, to fit bottle

1 Remove the basil leaves from the stems and discard the stems.

2 Wash the basil leaves and towel dry.

3 Place the leaves in a food processor and pulse until finely chopped.

4 Spoon the chopped basil into a clean bottle, then fill with oil to within ½ inch/1cm from the top. Replace the lid or use a cork to seal the bottle.

5 Shaking the bottle at least twice a day, let stand for 3 days. Strain out herbs, or for a more strongly flavored oil, do not strain. Add a sprig of basil to the bottle and reseal. After 3 days, store oil in the refrigerator, bringing it to room temperature before using.

Garlic Beet Oil

1 fresh beet (beetroot) with greens removed
6 garlic cloves, peeled
sunflower oil

1 Place beet and garlic in a small pan. Add enough oil to fill chosen bottle and simmer for 15 minutes. Let cool.

2 Using a sieve, pour the oil into the bottle and let stand for at least 48 hours. For a stronger garlic flavor, place a garlic clove in the bottle. Store oil in the refrigerator, bringing it to room temperature before using.

Cilantro Peppercorn Oil

1 Wash the cilantro and towel dry.

2 Place in a blender with enough oil to fill chosen bottle. Process until emulsified. Add peppercorns to the bottle, then pour in the cilantro oil. Replace the lid or use a cork to seal the bottle.

3 Shaking the bottle at least twice a day, let stand for 3 days. After 3 days, store oil in the refrigerator, bringing it to room temperature before using.

1 cup/15g fresh cilantro (coriander) leaves and tender stems

safflower (sunflower) oil

2–3 tbsp five-peppercorn blend

Dill and Chive Oil

1 Wash dill and chives and towel dry.

2 Place the dill in a food processor and pulse until finely chopped. Using scissors, snip chives into tiny pieces.

3 Spoon herbs into a bottle, then fill with oil to within ½ inch/1cm from top. Replace bottle lid or use a cork to seal bottle.

4 Shaking the bottle at least twice a day, let stand for 3 days. Add additional sprigs of dill to the bottle and reseal. Store oil in the refrigerator, bringing it to room temperature before using.

1 cup/30g fresh dill
½ cup/25g fresh chives or garlic chives
olive oil
additional sprigs of dill

Marigold Vinegar

sherry vinegar
organically grown marigold petals

1 In a small saucepan, heat the vinegar until warm, but not hot.

2 Remove the pan from the heat and add the marigold petals.

3 When cool, pour into a bottle. Let stand until the vinegar reaches desired shade of gold. Strain out the flower petals and pour the vinegar back into bottle. Use within one month.

Rosemary Vinegar

sprigs of fresh rosemary
white wine vinegar

1 Wash the rosemary and towel dry.

2 Place the sprigs in a bottle, then pour in the vinegar. Replace the bottle lid or use a cork to seal the bottle.

3 Let stand for 2 weeks or more before using. Use within one month.

Tarragon Vinegar

sprigs of fresh tarragon
white vinegar

1 Wash tarragon and towel dry.

2 Place the herbs in a bottle, then pour in vinegar. Replace the bottle lid or use a cork to seal bottle.

3 Let stand for 2 weeks or more before using. Use within one month.

Canning and Pickling

Barbara Jacksier delights in harvesting and preserving a variety of crops from her Virginia garden. "It allows me to enjoy the bounty throughout the year," she says. "I learned this long-established tradition from my great grandmother. It is a not only a healthy alternative—no need to use unnecessary additives—to buying pre-packed goods from the grocery store, but much more cost effective as well, not to mention the benefits to the environment. The jars are reusable, so you don't end up with old plastic or metal containers littering landfills."

It is extremely important to always follow recommended canning procedures to guarantee the safety of your home-canned foods.

Pickled Peppers

1 Wash and towel dry the peppers. Remove the stems and seeds and slice into thin rings.

2 Pack the pepper rings into canning jars, dividing them evenly.

3 In a saucepan, add the vinegars, water, salt, sugar, pickling spices, and garlic. Bring to a boil, then reduce heat and simmer for 15 minutes.

4 Pour liquid into the pepper-filled jars to within ½ inch/1cm of the top. Screw on the lids and process in a boiling water bath for 10 minutes. Remove jars and cool.

5 Let stand 3–4 weeks before using.

MAKES 4 x 1 PINT/500ML JARS

2 lb/900g red and yellow bell peppers

1 quart/1 liter cider vinegar

1 cup/240ml white vinegar

1 cup/240ml water

2 tbsp pickling salt

6 tbsp/85g granulated sugar

1 tbsp pickling spices tied into a cheesecloth (muslin) bag

2 garlic cloves, peeled

4 sterilized 1-pint/500ml canning jars

Pickled Cauliflower

1 Break the cauliflower into small florets, wash and towel dry.

2 Divide celery seeds evenly between all four jars.

3 In a saucepan, mix the water, vinegar, salt, and sugar. When the sugar and salt have dissolved, add cauliflower. Simmer for 2–3 minutes, then pour into jars to within ½ inch/1cm of the top. Screw on the lids and process in a boiling water bath for 10 minutes. Remove jars and cool.

4 Let stand 1–2 weeks before using.

MAKES 4 x 1 PINT/500ML JARS

2 small heads of cauliflower

1 tsp celery seeds

1 pint/480ml water

1 pint/480ml white vinegar

3 tbsp pickling salt

⅔ cup/140g granulated sugar

4 sterilized 1-pint/500ml canning jars

Sandwich Pickles

1 Wash and towel dry the cucumbers and cut into slices. Pack cucumber and onion slices into canning jars, dividing them evenly.

2 In a saucepan, mix the vinegars, salt, sugar, mustard seeds, and celery seeds. Heat, stirring until salt and sugar are dissolved, then pour into jars to within ½ inch/1cm of the top.

3 Screw on the lids and process in a boiling water bath for 10 minutes. Remove jars and cool.

4 Let stand 1–2 weeks before using.

MAKES 4 x 1 CUP/250ML JARS

5–6 lb/2.25–2.7kg pickling or Kirby cucumbers

½ cup/85g white onions, thinly sliced

1 cup/240ml white vinegar

½ cup/120ml cider vinegar

2 tbsp pickling salt

½ cup/115g granulated sugar

1 tsp mustard seeds

½ tsp celery seeds

4 sterilized 1 cup/250ml canning jars

Country Dill Pickles

1 Wash and towel dry the cucumbers and pack upright into canning jars, dividing them evenly. Do not over-pack as cucumbers will swell up as they "pickle." Divide the dill and mustard seeds evenly between the jars.

2 In a saucepan, mix the water, vinegar, and salt. Heat, stirring, until salt is dissolved, then pour into jars to within ½ inch/1cm of the top. Screw on the lids and process in a boiling water bath for 10 minutes. Remove jars and cool.

3 Let stand 1–2 weeks before using.

MAKES 4 x 1 QUART/1 LITER JARS

3–4 dozen pickling or Kirby cucumbers

12 large sprigs of dill

4 mature whole dill flower heads or 4 tbsp dill seeds, fresh or dried

1 tsp mustard seeds

1 quart/1 liter water

1 pint/480ml white vinegar

4 tbsp pickling salt

4 sterilized 1 quart/1 liter canning jars

Sweet Tomatoes

1 Plunge tomatoes into a large kettle of boiling water, then into a bowl of ice water; this will make peeling the tomatoes easy.

2 Peel the tomatoes, then pack into canning jars, dividing them evenly. Add 1 tbsp of lemon juice to each jar.

3 In a large pot, mix water, salt, and sugar. Heat, stirring, until the salt and sugar are dissolved, then pour into the jars to within ½ inch/1cm of the top. Screw on the lids and process in a pressure canner. Remove jars and cool.

MAKES 4 x 1 QUART/1 LITER JARS

3 dozen medium tomatoes

4 tbsp fresh lemon juice

1 pint/480ml water

1 tbsp sea salt

2 tsp granulated sugar

4 sterilized 1 quart/1 liter canning jars

Pickled Beets

Jennifer Rizzo inherited her love of gardening from her grandmother, Kay, the daughter of Hungarian tenant farmers. "When she married my grandfather, she carried her traditions with her. In the 1950s, on ¼ of an acre, she raised chickens, grew and canned all of her own produce, cooked the meat my grandfather hunted, and the fish he caught and smoked himself, and made everything from scratch. One of my fondest memories as a child was going to her house in the summer and eating raspberries straight off the canes or eating warm, garlicky pickles that had been brined in the sun, in an old crock with a plate on top weighed down with a rock. My pickled beet recipe started with her pickle recipe and has been tweaked for my own family's tastes. Grandma Kay passed away a few years ago at 98. I am proud to carry on her original farming/homesteading roots by growing my own vegetables organically. I even have some of her original raspberry canes and strawberry plants in my garden here in Illinois."

SERVES 6

2 lb/900g baby beets (beetroot)
2 cups/480ml water
1 cup/240ml white vinegar
½ cup/120ml red wine vinegar
½ cup/120ml apple cider vinegar
1 large onion, peeled and sliced
6–8 garlic cloves, peeled
2 cups/80g fresh dill, loosely torn
½–¾ cup/100–140g sugar

1 For easy peeling of the beets: in a large pan, add enough water to just cover beets and bring to a boil. Let boil for approximately 20 minutes. Drain the water and run the beets under cold water. Peel the beets and return to pan.

2 Add the water, vinegars, onion, garlic, dill, and sugar to the pan. Bring to a boil and reduce to a simmer. Simmer until the beets are fork tender, and remove from heat. Let the beets rest in the liquid until cool. Remove the dill. Using a slotted spoon, fill the two canning jars with the beets, onions, and garlic.

3 Add the cooking liquid to the jars until it reaches about 1 inch/2.5cm from the top of the jar. Seal with the lid and let sit overnight in the refrigerator for the flavors to develop. Pickled beets will keep for up to 3 weeks refrigerated.

Tips

The vinegar fumes can get quite strong when cooking, so it helps to open windows and run a fan.

Use baby beets as larger beets can be tougher and less flavorful.

The sugar, garlic, dill, and vinegar can be adjusted (more or less) to accommodate personal taste.

Using wide-mouth canning jars makes it easier to add or remove the beets.

Canning jars can be sterilized before filling by running them through the dishwasher cycle.

The true essentials of a feast are only fun and feed.

Oliver Wendell Holmes

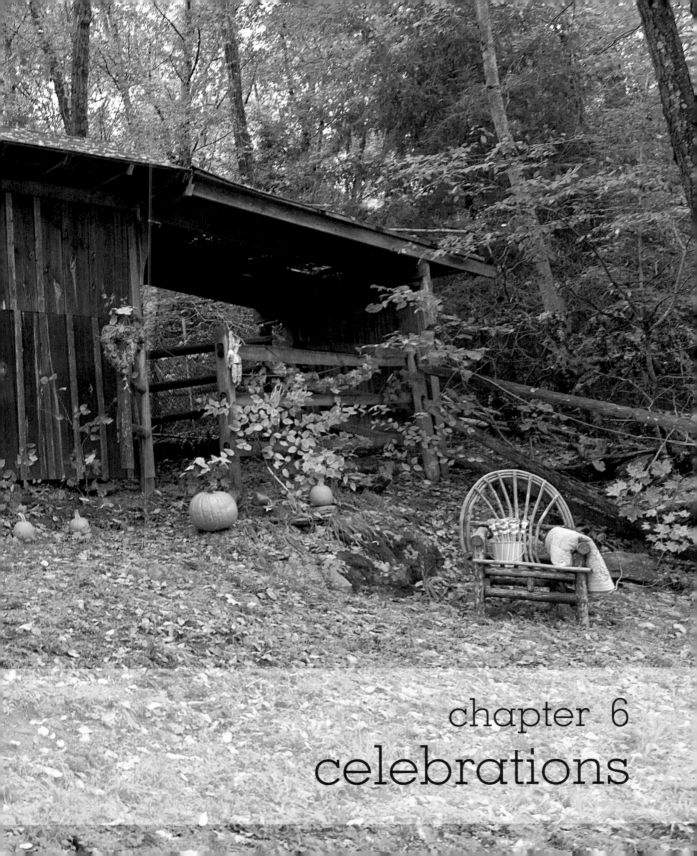

chapter 6
celebrations

HARVEST SUPPER

In 2000, Don and Debra Germain, along with their two teenagers, Nicole and Deg, found the home of their dreams in Woodbury, a small Connecticut town. The circa 1700s home that was once a cow barn came complete with over 18 acres of wooded bliss. The beautiful location inspired Debra and Don to hold a Harvest Pot Luck, an event to celebrate the arrival of autumn and get together with family, friends, and neighbors. Debra and Nicole work on getting the guest list, the menu, invitations, and decorations. "We plan the party many months in advance so everything goes smoothly," Debra says. And every year without fail, guests bring their favorite dish along with their appetite to enjoy a weekend of food and fun in the country. Mother and daughter also like to do something special for the children. This year, besides coming up with their own recipes for the adults and seasonal sweet treats for the kids, they fashioned hairpieces for the girls and supplied cowboy hats for the boys. Debra and Don's Harvest Pot Luck event serves much more than good, hearty food. It is a slice of life. One that nurtures friendships and preserves priceless memories.

Joe's Chicken Pot Pie

Not every boy is a budding chef but 11-year-old Joe O'Grady is a young man with a passion for cooking. Joe loves to create recipes using readily available items, among which is this easy two-crust chicken pie he contributed to the party. With a mix of vegetables, soup, and chicken, the simple dish makes a satisfying hearty main course perfect for a crisp autumn day. Feel free to substitute a variety of fresh or frozen mixed vegetables for the Veg-All.

SERVES 4

16-oz/450g can Veg-All (mixed vegetables)

3 chicken breasts, cooked and cut into bite-size pieces (about 2 cups/340g)

2 x 10-oz/280g cans cream of potato soup

2 ready-made pie crusts

1 Preheat the oven to 375°F/190°C/gas mark 5.

2 Unfold and lay out the bottom crust in an 8 inch/20cm pie plate. Spread with the Veg-All, then the chicken. Pour the cream of potato soup over the chicken. Top with the remaining crust, seal edges, and cut slits into the top to vent.

3 Bake for 45 minutes, until the crust is golden brown.

Deep-fried Turkey

One of the Germains' best-loved, and much anticipated, harvest pot luck courses is Don's deep-fried turkey, a recipe and method original to Louisiana. "The deep frying process creates a flash-frying effect that seals in the juices, resulting in flavorful and tender meat and a perfectly crispy golden skin without any oily aftertaste. The cajun rub adds just the right kick," Don explains. Though it requires a deep-fryer made specifically for this purpose, it's well worth the investment as the process is much less time-consuming than roasting in a conventional oven or rotisserie. This is a method of cooking turkey that has become extremely popular in the US in the last few years. Do not attempt to make it unless you have a turkey deep-fryer and follow the instructions exactly.

SERVES 7–10

15-17 lb/ 6.8–7.7kg fresh turkey
corn oil (see below)
8-oz/225g pack Cajun seasoning
turkey deep-fryer

1 The day before cooking, remove the giblets from the turkey's cavity. Clean the turkey inside and out by running it under cold water. Pat dry.

2 Sprinkle the turkey inside and out with Cajun seasoning. Cover the turkey in foil and refrigerate overnight.

3 When ready to fry: remove the foil from the turkey and follow the deep fryer instructions, approximately 3½ minutes per pound/8 minutes per kg at 325°F/160°C.

Tip

Your turkey deep-fryer instructions will tell you how much oil you will need.

Creamy Sweet Potatoes

On their own, sweet potatoes are naturally delicious. But mixed with milk and sugar they acquire a melt-in-your-mouth texture that's hard to beat. "Adding a bit of vanilla and a topping of a crunchy blend of almonds, pecans, and crusty brown sugar elevate the humble yams to a delicacy," Debra says.

SERVES 10

5 lb/2.3kg sweet potatoes, peeled and cooked
4 eggs, lightly beaten
1 cup/225g granulated sugar
½ cup/120ml milk
2 sticks/115g butter, softened
1 tsp vanilla extract (essence)

For the topping:
1 cup/225g brown sugar
½ cup/55g all-purpose (plain) flour
1 cup/115g chopped pecans
1 cup/115g chopped almonds
5 tbsp/70g butter

1 Preheat the oven to 350°F/180°C/gas mark 4.

2 In a large bowl, mash the cooked sweet potatoes. Add the eggs, sugar, milk, butter, and vanilla extract; mix well. Transfer the mixture to a greased 3-quart/3-liter baking dish.

3 In another bowl, mix the brown sugar with the flour, pecans, almonds, and butter. Spread over the sweet potato mixture.

4 Bake for 35–40 minutes, or until the sides begin to bubble.

Sausage, Apple, and Sauerkraut Casserole

Debra's version of this classic old-world favorite brings together flavors and sustenance. The brown sugar mellows out the tartness of the sauerkraut, potatoes and apples provide texture, and the sausage brings the perfect meaty balance to this hearty German-inspired dish.

SERVES 12

4 lb/1.8kg Kielbasa or other sausage, sliced

10 unpeeled red potatoes (3½–4 lb/1.6–1.8kg), cubed

27-oz/750-g jar sauerkraut, drained

8 medium McIntosh (Granny Smith) apples, unpeeled and sliced

1 lb/450g brown sugar

1 Preheat the oven to 375°F/190°C/gas mark 5.

2 In an ovenproof Dutch oven (casserole), layer half the sausage, then all the potatoes, sauerkraut, apples, and brown sugar in that order, then finish with a layer of sausage.

3 Cover and bake for 35 minutes or until bubbles begin to appear on the sides. Uncover and bake for an additional 10 minutes.

Butternut Squash and Apple Casserole

Beth Zaskey's butternut squash and apple casserole blends a tasty and unexpected combination of flavors, and this easy-to-prepare side dish is a seasonal favorite. The walnuts add a bit of crunch and the raisins a touch of chewiness to the mellow texture of the apples and the squash.

1 Preheat the oven to 350°F/180°C/gas mark 4.

2 Toss together the squash and apples in large bowl.

3 In a separate bowl, stir together the melted butter and brown sugar. Add the raisins and walnuts. Pour the mixture over the squash and apples. Stir until well coated and pour into a shallow baking pan.

4 Bake uncovered for 1 hour or until the squash is tender. Serve hot. For a sweeter touch, add a light drizzle of maple syrup.

SERVES 6

1 large butternut squash, peeled, seeded, and diced

2 tart apples, peeled, cored, and diced

4 tbsp/55g butter, melted

½ cup/115g brown sugar

4 tbsp raisins

4 tbsp chopped walnuts

maple syrup, to taste (optional)

Potato Salad

Since potato salad was introduced to America by German immigrants in the mid-19th century, it has become a popular choice for casual get-togethers and a staple of Debra Germain's autumn feast. This versatile side dish lends itself to numerous varieties of dressings, but Debra favors her family's sweet and spicy version of the classic dish.

1 Boil the potatoes until tender, but not mushy. Set aside.

2 Boil the eggs until hard boiled. Peel the eggs, slice, and set aside.

3 In a large bowl, mix the potatoes, eggs, onion, and celery.

4 In another bowl, combine the mayonnaise, relish, mustard, and horseradish. Mix well and add to the potato mixture. Blend well and refrigerate until serving.

SERVES 8

10 unpeeled red potatoes (3½–4 lb/ 1.6–1.8kg), cubed

2 medium red onions, peeled and chopped

4 celery sticks, finely chopped

7 eggs

1 cup/225g mayonnaise

2 heaping tbsp sweet relish (cucumber pickle)

2 heaping tbsp spicy brown mustard

2 heaping tbsp horseradish

Tip

For best results prepare one day ahead.

Nana Barrett's Cornbread

SERVES 12

1 tbsp corn oil

1 stick/115g butter, at room temperature

½ cup/115g sugar

2 medium eggs, separated (first eggs of the morning are best, but eggs at room temperature will do just fine)

1 cup/115g all-purpose (plain) flour

2½ tsp baking powder

pinch of salt

1 cup/240ml milk, at room temperature

1 cup/150g cornmeal (polenta)

Corn, also know as maize, was a staple of Native Americans' meals long before European settlers learned how to incorporate the grain in their diet, mostly to bake cornmeal breads. Dee Byrnes, one of Debra Germain's guests, inherited her cornbread recipe from her Nana, Helen Barrett. Back when it was first written, over a century ago, the recipe called for collecting the first eggs of the day while still warm and using warm milk—"warm" being the key word for this delightful old-fashioned bread. But, keeping in mind that not everyone has access to eggs-fresh-from-the-coop or has a cow that can be milked at the crack of dawn, eggs and milk at room temperature are perfectly acceptable substitutes.

1 Preheat the oven to 400°F/200°C/gas mark 6.

2 Grease a 10-inch/25cm cast iron skillet (frying pan) with the corn oil.

3 In a bowl, cream the butter and sugar together. Add the egg yolks and mix well.

4 In another bowl, whisk the egg whites until stiff, but not dry, and set aside.

5 Add the flour, baking powder, and salt to the creamed mixture slowly, then add the milk slowly, mixing well after each addition. Add the cornmeal to the mixture, and let stand for about 5 minutes.

6 Gently fold in the egg whites. Pour into the greased skillet and bake for 30–35 minutes, until the top is lightly browned.

7 Remove from the skillet and cut into 12 portions.

Pumpkin Cream Cheese Nut Bread

Lynn Brewer's pumpkin bread is an autumn must-have. Its tantalizing aroma is matched by the sweet, moist texture of pumpkin and complementary spices. Lynn serves it to her family for breakfast but also as a midday snack with a glass of milk or a hot cup of tea. No matter when you offer it, this flavorful bread is a satisfying treat any time of the day.

1 Preheat the oven to 350°F/180°C/gas mark 4.

2 In a large bowl, combine the sugar, cream cheese, and butter; mix until well-blended. Add eggs one at a time, mixing well between each addition. Add the pumpkin and blend well.

3 In another bowl, combine the flour, baking soda, salt, cinnamon, baking powder, cloves, nutmeg, and orange zest. Mix well, then add to the egg mixture blending all until just moistened. Fold in the walnuts.

4 Pour mixture into two greased and floured 2 lb/900g loaf pans. Bake for 1 hour 10 minutes, or until a wooden toothpick inserted in the center of the loaves comes out clean. Let the loaves cool for 10 minutes before removing from the pans. Transfer the loaves to a wire rack to cool completely.

MAKES 2 LOAVES

2½ cups/560g granulated sugar

1 cup/225g cream cheese, softened

1 stick/115g butter

4 eggs

16 oz/450g canned pumpkin

3½ cups/400g all-purpose (plain) flour

2 tsp baking soda (bicarbonate of soda)

1 tsp salt

1 tsp ground cinnamon

½ tsp baking powder

¼ tsp ground cloves

¼ tsp grated nutmeg

1 tbsp finely grated orange zest

1 cup/115g chopped walnuts

Pumpkin Cake Roll

SERVES 6–8

3 eggs

1 cup/225g sugar

1 tsp fresh lemon juice

⅔ cup/140g canned spiced organic pumpkin (see tip)

¾ cup/85g all-purpose (plain) flour

1 tsp baking powder

pinch of sea salt

4 tbsp (or a little more) sunflower seeds

For the filling:

1 cup/115g confectioners' (icing) sugar

¾ cup/170g cream cheese, softened

4 tbsp soft butter

½ tsp vanilla extract (essence)

As sure as the first fall leaves appear, iconic pumpkins show up everywhere—from farm stands, farmers' markets, and supermarkets to garden centers. And when it comes to autumn's recipes—from starters to desserts—these much-loved members of the squash family are as versatile as they are flavorful and nutritious. Seasonal spices like cinnamon, nutmeg, and cloves contribute to the fragrant aroma of this pumpkin cake, while the cream cheese filling adds a smooth counterpoint to the crunch of the sunflower seeds. Whether rounding up a harvest meal, or offered as a snack with a hot cup of tea, this elegant cake is a delicious alternative to pumpkin pie, and a mainstay of Robin O'Grady's autumn menu.

1 Preheat the oven to 375°F/190°C/gas mark 5.

2 With an electric beater, beat the eggs for 5 full minutes. Beat in the sugar, then stir in the lemon juice and pumpkin.

3 Stir together the flour, baking powder, and salt and fold into the pumpkin mixture.

Tip

If spiced pumpkin is unavailable, simply add
1 tsp ground cinnamon, ½ tsp ground ginger,
⅛ tsp grated nutmeg, ⅛ tsp ground cloves,
and ⅛ tsp allspice to the plain canned pumpkin.

4 Spread the mixture in a greased
15 x 10 x 1 inch/38 x 25 x 2.5cm pan, lined
with greased wax (greaseproof) paper.
Sprinkle on the sunflower seeds. Bake for
15 minutes.

5 Remove the cake from the oven, carefully
flip/turn the pan onto a sheet of wax paper
slightly larger than the cake pan, dusted with
confectioners' sugar. Carefully lift the pan
off the cake, then carefully peel off the wax
paper, and let it cool.

6 Mix together the filling ingredients and
gently spread over the cake. Starting with
one of the short ends, carefully roll the cake
into a log shape, like a jelly roll (roulade).
Lightly sprinkle more confectioners' sugar on
the cake roll (optional). The sunflower seeds
side will be on the outside of the cake roll.

Chunky Chocolate Chip Cookies

Crunchy nuts and chocolate chips are a heavenly match bursting with flavors. Sami Hollman's famous chunky cookies are Debra Germain's younger guests' favorite sweet treat. Sami advises: "Bake plenty because the kids eat them up fast!"

MAKES 24–28 COOKIES

2¼ cups/250g all-purpose (plain) flour
1 tsp salt
1 tsp baking soda (bicarbonate of soda)
2 sticks/225g butter
¾ cup/170g granulated sugar
¾ cup/170g brown sugar
1 tsp vanilla extract (essence)
2 large eggs
1⅔ cups/280g chocolate chips
1 cup/115g chopped nuts (optional)

1 Preheat the oven to 375°F/190°C/gas mark 5.

2 Sift the salt and baking soda with the flour.

3 Put the butter and sugars in a large bowl. Beat until smooth. Stir in the vanilla extract. Add the eggs and beat until they are completely incorporated. Mix in the flour a little at a time. Add the chocolate chips and chopped nuts making sure to stir them well into the batter. Do not use an electric mixer.

4 Drop 1 tbsp of the mixture onto cookie sheets for each cookie, spacing well apart.

5 Bake for 9–11 minutes. Let cool for 2–3 minutes before removing the cookies from the cookie sheet. Transfer the cookies to a wire rack to cool completely.

Marshmallow Treats

Making these treats is easy and fun. Debra is in charge of melting the chocolate candy, but her grandchildren delight in helping assemble the colorful gumdrops and marshmallows and selecting the sprinkles and nuts. "I like to let them use their imagination and creativity," Debra says. "The beauty of these treats is that they can be adapted to any theme celebration or holiday by simply changing the color of the chocolate and the choice of finishing touches."

MAKES 12 SKEWERS

12 wooden skewers, sharp tip cut off
1 large bag of multicolor marshmallows
1 large bag of gumdrops (fruit gums)
7 oz/200g microwaveable candy melt chocolate (follow package direction for melting)
assorted sprinkles (hundreds and thousands) and chopped nuts

1 For each "marshmallow treat": begin by threading one marshmallow on a skewer, then a gumdrop, followed by 2 more marshmallows. Dip the top marshmallow in melted chocolate then in the sprinkles and nuts.

2 Set the completed skewer in a glass until the candy hardens, about 5–8 minutes. Repeat until all the skewers are done.

Candy Apples

MAKES 8

8 apples, washed and dried

1 cup/240ml water

3 cups/675g sugar

½ cup/115g light corn (golden) syrup

4 tbsp red hot candies (see tip)

½ tsp red food coloring

assorted toppings (coconut, colored sprinkles, nuts)

Apple harvest and candy apples (also known as toffee apples) go hand in hand. This classic autumn treat is a fun and simple project for children to prepare under adult supervision. It requires careful attention because the candy coating becomes hot during the cooking process. Using a variety of food coloring and toppings for the coating allows for creative ways to match any theme or occasion. A layer of crunchy candylike syrup coats crisp, tart apples in this timeless favorite. For a fun look, Nicole Germain-Perez (Debra's daughter) suggests substituting chopsticks, popsicle sticks, or skewers with sturdy twigs tied with colorful ribbons.

1 Insert sticks into the apples.

2 Grease a cookie sheet.

3 In a 2 quart/2 liter saucepan, combine the remaining ingredients except for the toppings. Bring to a boil without stirring. Continue to boil until a candy thermometer reads 290°F/145°C, about 20 minutes. If you do not have a candy thermometer, you can test by dropping a little bit of the mixture into cold water; if it separates into thin threads, it's ready.

4 Remove from the heat. Dip each apple into the syrupy mixture and roll in the topping of your choice. If the syrup starts to harden, set the pan over low heat.

5 Place the candied apples on the greased cookie sheet. Cool 1 hour before serving.

Tip

These cinnamon-flavored hard sweets can be bought online in the UK from www.everything cinnamon.co.uk

Candy Corn Popcorn Balls

Festive yet frugal, sweet and gooey Candy Corn Popcorn Balls are the perfect treats for autumn celebrations, especially for trick-or-treating. They are a cinch to make with melted marshmallows, popcorn, and candy corn. Nicole always enlists the help of her little daughters Stella, 7 Maci, 3, and Fibi, 2 in making the crunchy confections.

1 Microwave the butter and marshmallows in a large microwave bowl on high for 1½–2 minutes or until the marshmallows are puffed. Stir in the gelatin until well mixed. Pour the mixture over the popcorn and candy corn. Mix lightly until well coated.

2 Shape into 15 balls with greased or wet hands. Set the finished balls on wax (greaseproof) paper and let dry completely before serving.

Tips

Jelly crystals can be bought in UK at Holland & Barrett. If using a colored gelatin, popcorn balls will be slightly colored.

Candy corn can be bought online in UK from www.americansweets.co.uk

MAKES 15

½ stick/55g butter

1 pack (10½ oz/300g) miniature marshmallows

3-oz/85-g pack gelatin dessert (jelly crystals), any flavor/color

12 cups popped popcorn (⅔ cup/140g unpopped)

1 cup/225g candy corn (see tips)

CHRISTMAS

I met my friend Judi Gallagher (an honors graduate of the Culinary Arts Program at Johnson & Wales College), many years ago when I owned restaurants in Florida. Over the years, our shared passion for food resulted in cooking and hosting many dinner parties together. As Judi says: "The taste of certain dishes can transport you back to another time and place. Some of our most memorable experiences involve a kitchen table overflowing with comfort food and there is a distinctive relationship between different parts of the world and food."

With that in mind, every year around the Christmas holidays, Judi and I get together to cook up a meal that brings back fond memories and reflects various areas where we both have lived. In this instance, because of the many years I spent in Canada, a country that will remain close to my heart forever, we opted for some dishes that pay tribute to French Canadian cuisine. But, since I am equally infatuated with America and it is Judi's homeland, we also included some regional favorites. Both Judi and I are fond of locally grown food and we make weekly trips to our farmer's market to gather whatever is in season. Cooking together is not only a fun and delicious experience, but taking in our guests' enjoyment is the best reward.

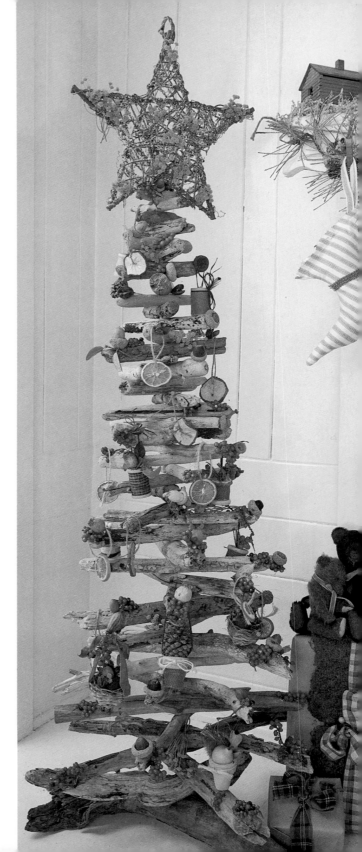

Tourtiere (Canadian Meat Pie)

For me, the word "tourtiere" means much more than food. It instantly brings back the many magical Christmases I spent in Canada. The traditional meat pie was a staple of the holidays, a simple but filling dish my boys devoured with great gusto. I still think of the meaty pie with a crunchy golden crust as comfort food par excellence, which stirs up visions of my little children's innocent faces flushed from playing in the pristine icy snow drifts, and their hungry enthusiasm digging into the steaming tourtiere. I make this dish every Christmas and every bite wraps me up in the memory of those happy days like a warm wooly blanket on a freezing winter night.

SERVES 8

1½ lb/675g lean ground (minced) pork
1 large onion, chopped finely
¾ cup/180ml water
2 large potatoes, cooked and mashed
¼ tsp ground cinnamon
¼ tsp ground allspice
¼ tsp ground cloves
store-bought pastry for a two-crust pie
sea salt and ground black pepper

1 Preheat the oven to 400°F/200°C/gas mark 6.

2 In a pan, combine the pork, onion, and water and cook over low heat for 2 hours, stirring occasionally. Remove from the heat, and add salt and pepper to taste. Add the mashed potatoes and spices and mix well.

3 Place the meat filling in the pastry crust. Top with upper crust.

4 Bake for 10 minutes. Reduce the oven temperature to 375°F/190°C/gas mark 5 and bake for an additional 20 minutes. Serve hot.

Buffalo Roast

SERVES 8

1 tbsp paprika

2 tsp sea salt

1 tsp garlic powder

½ tsp dried oregano, crushed

½ tsp dried thyme, crushed

½ tsp garlic salt

ground black pepper

½ tsp onion powder

½ tsp cayenne pepper

2 tbsp olive oil

3–4 lb/1.4–1.6kg boneless bison sirloin tip roast (joint)

roasted root vegetables (see opposite), to serve

Long ago, buffaloes roamed the North American grasslands and the Canadian prairies, and were prized for their meat as well as for providing clothing and spiritual inspiration. Back then, the magnificent beasts were so numerous that the great herds prompted this description from early explorers "As if the plains were black and appeared as if in motion." Through the 1800s, buffaloes were hunted for their fur and meat with disastrous results. Today they are raised on private and public land. Their meat, sweet and low in fat, offers half the calories and cholesterol, and requires less cooking time, making it a tasty and healthy alternative to traditional red meats. A rub of oil and herb blend keeps the meat moist while infusing the roast with aromatic flavor. Nutrient-packed root vegetables add yet more delicious and healthy benefits to this easy, satisfying dish.

1 Preheat the oven to 375°F/190°C/gas mark 5.

2 In a small bowl, combine the paprika, salt, garlic powder, oregano, thyme, garlic salt, black pepper, onion powder, and cayenne pepper. Stir in the oil until well combined.

3 Place the meat on a rack in a shallow roasting pan. Spread the seasoned oil over the surface of the meat and insert a meat thermometer into the center of the meat.

4 Roast for 15 minutes. Reduce the oven temperature to 300°F/150°C/gas mark 2. Roast until the meat thermometer registers 140°F/60°C.

5 Remove from the oven, cover the roast tightly with aluminum foil and let stand in the pan on a wire rack for 15 minutes. The temperature of the meat after standing should be 145°F/63°C (medium rare).

6 Slice the meat thinly across the grain and serve with the roasted root vegetables opposite.

Roasted Celery Root, Beets and Turnips

1 Preheat the oven to 375°F/190°C/gas mark 5.

2 Place the beets in the oven to roast.

3 Spread the turnips and celery root on a baking sheet, toss with oil and seasoning, and roast, turning 2–3 times until mostly tender, about 40 minutes. Remove the vegetables from the oven.

4 Remove the foil from the beets. Cut into wedges; the skin will peel right off as the guests cut into them.

SERVES 8

3 beets (beetroots), skins washed, each individually wrapped in aluminum foil

2 celery root (celeriac) bulbs, peeled and cut into small cubes

2–3 large turnips, peeled and cut into small cubes

olive oil

fresh thyme

sea salt and ground black pepper

Tip

You may also roast the turnip and celery root with the buffalo in the roasting pan for added flavor (see left).

Pea Soup

SERVES 6

1½ cups/200g green split peas

¼ stick/30g butter

1 large onion, peeled and chopped

2–3 celery sticks, chopped

1 cup/170g chopped carrots

1½ lb/675g smoked pork hocks (trotters)

2 tsp dried marjoram

1 large garlic clove, peeled and chopped

2 quarts/2 liters water

sea salt and ground black pepper

Judi's familiarity with pea soup stems from her days in New England. Mine goes back to my life in Canada. The New England version features green peas while the Canadian uses yellow ones. But, whether you use one type or the other, this hearty, flavor-packed soup is the answer to bone-chilling winter days, wherever you are. To add a touch of holiday flair, just garnish with star-shaped croutons quick-fried in olive oil and sprinkled with dried thyme.

1 Wash and drain the peas.

2 Melt the butter in a large stockpot or Dutch oven over medium–high heat. Add the onion, celery, and carrots. Sauté until the vegetables begin to soften, about 8 minutes. Add the pork, marjoram and garlic; stir 1 minute. Add peas, then water, and bring to a boil. Reduce the heat to medium–low. Partially cover the pot; simmer soup until the pork and vegetables are tender, and peas are falling apart, stirring often, about 1 hour 10 minutes.

3 Transfer the hocks to a bowl.

4 Purée the soup in batches in a blender, then return the purée to the pot.

5 Cut the pork off the bones, dice the meat, and return to the soup. Season with salt and pepper. Serve hot.

Herb Croutons

MAKES 12 SMALL CROUTONS

12 slices sandwich bread
olive oil, for frying
dried thyme, for sprinkling
sea salt and ground black pepper

1 Stamp out 12 stars from the bread with a small star cookie cutter.

2 Pour olive oil in a heavy skillet (frying pan) (enough to cover about 6 stars, depending on the size of the skillet) and heat oil over medium–high heat.

3 Carefully add croutons (best to do this in two batches), spread out in a single layer and quick-fry until golden, then turn over to fry the other side.

4 Remove the croutons from the oil with a slotted spoon and let drain on a paper towel (kitchen paper). Sprinkle with dried thyme, and salt and pepper. Repeat with the second batch, adding oil if necessary. Alternatively, you can gently toss the croutons with olive oil, thyme, and salt and pepper in a bowl and toast in a 350°F/180°C/gas mark 4 oven on a cookie sheet until golden brown.

Fried Green Tomatoes

Though fried green tomatoes were made famous by the 1991 movie of the same name (based on Fannie Flagg's 1988 novel Fried Green Tomatoes at the Whistle Stop Cafe), *the culinary delight goes back to the early 1800s, and unlike popular belief, originated from the Midwest, not the deep South. But, whether prepared in the northern tradition with bread crumbs, or the southern way with cornmeal, the crunchy saltiness of the fried bread, combined with the fresh tartness of the unripe fruit, conspires to give this country dish its originality and mouth-watering texture. Serve it with eggs for a hearty breakfast, or as an accompaniment for fish, poultry, or meat for a memorable main course.*

SERVES 4

1 large egg, lightly beaten
½ cup/120ml buttermilk
½ cup/55g all-purpose (plain) flour
½ cup/70g cornmeal (or 55g bread crumbs)
1 tsp sea salt
½ tsp ground black pepper
a pinch of chili powder
a pinch of dried thyme
3 medium-size green tomatoes, cut into ⅓-inch/.75cm slices
vegetable oil for frying
sea salt to taste

1 In a bowl, combine the egg and buttermilk; set aside. In a shallow bowl combine 4 tbsp flour, cornmeal, salt, pepper, chili powder, and thyme.

2 Dredge the tomato slices in the remaining flour; dip in the egg mixture, and dredge in the cornmeal mixture.

3 Pour oil to a depth of ¼–½ inch/ 5mm–1cm in a large cast iron skillet (frying pan); heat to 375°F/190°C. Drop the tomatoes, in batches, into the hot oil, and cook for 2 minutes on each side, or until golden. Drain on paper towels (kitchen paper) or a rack. Sprinkle the hot tomatoes with salt.

Hoecakes with Chipotle Sour Cream

One of Judi's fondest childhood memories is waking up to the smell of hot cornmeal biscuits wafting from the family's kitchen every Sunday morning. These "hoecakes," as they are called, owe their name to the manner in which they were originally cooked by farmhands on the wide-blade of a cultivating hoe heated on a fire. Long gone are those days, but the popularity of the humble hoecakes live on, though, today, they are cooked in a hot cast iron skillet (frying pan) on the stovetop (hob). However, rather than keeping them warm in the oven until serving time, Judi pays tribute to the old tradition by setting them over an upside-down skillet set over a heated burner. Hoecakes with a pat of butter, a little jam, a drizzle of honey, or maple syrup make delicious breakfast fare, or served plain, are the perfect substitute for bread at any meal. For a savory touch, Judi serves them with a dab of sour cream spiced up with chipotle.

1 In a bowl, mix all the ingredients, except for the frying oil.

2 Heat the frying oil in a large cast iron skillet (frying pan) over medium heat.

3 Drop 2 tbsp batter per cake into the hot skillet.

4 Fry each hoecake until brown and crisp; turn with a spatula, and then brown the other side.

5 Transfer the hoecakes to a plate lined with paper towel (kitchen paper) to drain.

6 Prepare the topping. Blend the sour cream and mashed pepper together well.

7 Serve the hot hoecakes topped with chipotle sour cream.

SERVES 4

For the hoecakes:

1 cup/115g self-rising flour

1 cup/140g self-rising cornmeal (polenta) or ⅞ cup/125g cornmeal + 2 tsp baking powder + ½ tsp salt

2 eggs

1 tbsp sugar

¾ cup/180ml buttermilk

6 tbsp water

4 tbsp vegetable oil

about 4 tbsp canola (rapeseed) oil, for frying

For the topping:

1 cup/225g sour cream

1 chipotle pepper, mashed, juice drained

Sour Cream Cake with Apple Compote

Though the term "American Melting Pot" refers to the vast and varied origins of the immigrants who made up (and still make) the country's rich and colorful tapestry, it is a most appropriate description of its culinary landscape as well. Among those who brought with them recipes from their homelands, Jewish cooks were the first to create many of the cakes still enjoyed today. Though a number of original recipes have been adapted to modern cuisine, the classic sour cream cake remains a favorite and is as popular as apple pie. According to tradition, Judi serves her sour cream cake with a heaping side of apple compote for holiday brunch festivities, but the moist cake and topping make a sweet treat any time of the year (or day).

SERVES 10–12

1½ sticks/170g unsalted butter

¾ cup/170g granulated sugar

3 eggs, beaten

¾ cup/170g sour cream

1 tbsp vanilla extract (essence)

2 cups/225g unbleached all-purpose (plain) flour

2 tsp baking powder

½ tsp salt

For the streusel:

½ cup/115g brown sugar

2 cups/225g pecans, chopped

1 tbsp ground cinnamon

1 Preheat the oven to 350°F/180°C/gas mark 4.

2 Grease and lightly flour a 10-inch/25cm bundt pan or two 8 x 4 x 2 inch/2 lb/900g loaf pans.

3 In a bowl, cream together the butter and granulated sugar. Add the beaten eggs and blend. Add the sour cream and vanilla and mix well.

4 In another bowl, sift together flour, baking powder, and salt. Fold the dry ingredients into the creamed mixture and beat until blended. Do not overmix.

5 In a separate bowl, mix the brown sugar, chopped pecans, and cinnamon together.

6 Pour half of the batter into the prepared pan. Sprinkle half the brown sugar mixture on top. Pour the remaining batter into the pan over the brown sugar mixture. Repeat the process with the remaining brown sugar mixture.

7 Place in the preheated oven on the middle rack for about 60 minutes, or until a wooden toothpick inserted into the center of the cake comes out clean.

8 Let rest for about 45 minutes and serve while still warm with warm apple compote.

Apple Compote

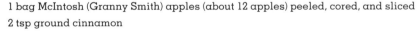

1 bag McIntosh (Granny Smith) apples (about 12 apples) peeled, cored, and sliced

2 tsp ground cinnamon

⅓ cup/70g sugar

4 tbsp Calvados (apple brandy)

4 tbsp water (if needed for apples)

Put all the ingredients in a pan over medium heat. Mash the apples as they cook, adding more water if needed, and cook until soft and chunky, about 25 minutes. Serve warm.

Lost Bread

Growing up in Paris, it goes without saying that Lost Bread (pain perdu) was a regular and much-loved breakfast item and after-school snack in our home. My mom made it in the traditional French way with stale bread sliced on the bias and dipped into a mixture of eggs and milk, then fried in butter to a crusty golden exterior enveloping a smooth-as-velvet filling. A dusting of powdered sugar was, so to speak, the icing on the cake. Later on, when I lived in Canada, I made the recipe exactly like my mother taught me, but added my own touch with a drizzle of warm maple syrup. Even now, whenever I taste the delectable and oh-so-easy to make bread, it takes me back to my mom's loving ways and I am 10 years old again.

SERVES 6–8

3 eggs
1 cup/225g sugar
1 cup/240ml whole milk
1 tsp vanilla extract (essence)
1 loaf stale French bread, cut into 1½ inch/4cm slices
butter, for griddle pan
confectioners' (icing) sugar, for dusting
warm maple syrup (to taste)

1 Preheat a nonstick griddle pan over medium heat.

2 In a large bowl, whisk the eggs well, add the sugar and whisk again. Add milk and vanilla extract. Stir well.

3 Dip the bread thoroughly in the egg-milk mixture one slice at a time. Lightly butter the griddle pan. Add 2–3 bread slices to the pan and cook slowly, 3 or 4 minutes on each side or until the bread is golden brown and the edges are slightly crunchy. Repeat until all bread slices are done.

4 Dust bread with confectioners' sugar and drizzle with warm maple syrup. Serve immediately.

Settler's Sugar Pie

This traditional sweet-as-candy sugar pie is one of Quebec's most famous desserts and a fitting ending to a festive menu. The delicious regional treat's crunchy caramel-like filling is sure to please lovers of sweets. Serve small portions with fresh whipped cream: a little slice goes a long way.

SERVES 8–10

unbaked 9½-inch/24cm tart shell
1½ cups/340g brown sugar
2 tbsp all-purpose (plain) flour
⅛ tsp salt
1 tsp vanilla extract (essence)
⅓ cup/75ml heavy (double) cream
whipped cream, to serve

1 Set an oven rack in the middle position. Preheat the oven to 350°F/180°C/gas mark 4.

2 Wearing disposable gloves, use your hands to combine the sugar, flour, and salt in a mixing bowl. Pick out and discard any hard particles of brown sugar. Sprinkle the mixture evenly over the bottom of the tart shell.

3 In another bowl, add the vanilla extract to the heavy cream, mixing well. Pour over the sugar mixture, spreading lightly with a spatula.

4 Bake for approximately 35 minutes, or until the pastry is golden brown and the filling is dark and bubbling. Remove from the oven and cool on a wire rack.

5 Serve either slightly warm or at room temperature with a dollop of fresh whipped cream.

Tip

This tart is best when eaten the day it is baked. Store leftovers loosely covered with a paper towel (kitchen paper) and wax (greaseproof) paper in the refrigerator.

Spiced Candied Walnuts

MAKES 4 CUPS/450G

4 cups/450g walnut halves

1 cup/115g confectioners' (icing) sugar, sifted

canola (rapeseed) oil, for frying

½ tsp cayenne pepper

½ tsp ground cinnamon

pinch of sea salt

¼ tsp ground black pepper

Spiced nuts make a great snack, and packed in pretty glass jars, plastic bags, or any attractive airtight containers, a lovely gift. The sweet and spicy mix also adds a distinctive crunch to salads and vegetables. These flavorful morsels are highly addictive, so make plenty to have on hand through the holiday season.

1 Bring a large pan of water to a boil. Add the walnuts and blanch for 30 seconds. Drain and transfer the nuts to a medium bowl. While the nuts are still hot and slightly wet, add the confectioners' sugar and toss to coat the nuts. Stir and toss until all the sugar has melted into the nuts; if bits of unmelted sugar remain on the nuts, they will not fry properly. Stir the nuts again before frying.

2 In a large, heavy-based skillet (frying pan), heat about 1 inch/2.5cm oil to 350°F/180°C.

3 Using a large slotted spoon, transfer a few nuts to the hot oil, allowing the foam to subside before adding another spoonful (otherwise, the oil could foam over and burn you). Fry in small batches until the nuts are medium brown, about 45 seconds; be careful not to overcook. Scatter on an unlined baking sheet to cool slightly.

4 In a small bowl, stir together the cayenne pepper, cinnamon, salt, and pepper.

5 While the nuts are still warm, transfer them to a bowl and sprinkle evenly with about half of the spice mix. Toss well to coat, and then taste a nut. Add more spice mix to taste, tossing well after each addition.

6 When cool, pack in an airtight jar. The nuts will keep at room temperature for at least 2 weeks.

INDEX

SOURCES

Visit the wonderful places that provided props, locations, and services during the creation of *The Romantic Prairie Cookbook*.

California
A Beautiful Mess (Agoura Hills)
www.abeautifulmessantiques.com

Biglieri Farms Farm Market
17815 E. Hwy 88, Clements,
CA 95227

Farmhouse Inn
www.farmhouseinn.com

Hooverville Orchard (Placerville)
www.hoovervilleorchards.com

Ramekins (Sonoma)
www.ramekins.com

Summer Cottage Antiques (Petaluma)
www.summercottageantiques.com

The Agoura Antique Mart
www.agouraantiquemart.com

Tumbleweed and Dandelion (Venice)
www.tumbleweedanddandelion.com

Connecticut
Clyde's Cider Mill
www.BFClydescidermill.com

Nest
80 Stonington Road, Mystic,
CT 06355
(860) 536-5400

Vermont
Fat Toad Farm
www.fattoadfarm.com

Vermont Harvest Folk Art
www.vermontharvestfolkart.com

New Hampshire
Berrybogg Farm
www.berryboggfarm.com

New York
Raspberry Fields Farm
www.raspberryfieldsfarm.com

Virginia
Ekster Antiques
www.eksterantiques.com

USA
Pottery Barn
www.potterybarn.com

Restoration Hardware
www.restorationhardware.com

Williams Sonoma
www.williams-sonoma.com

AUTHOR'S ACKNOWLEDGMENTS

Coming up with a book concept—may it be interiors, gardens, or, in this instance, cookery—is easy enough. Translating the concept into a tangible product is another issue. One that cannot be accomplished without the help of skilled professionals and willing participants.

As with my first book (*Romantic Prairie Style*), I have had the pleasure to work again with photographer Mark Lohman, Cico's publishers Cindy Richards and David Peters, and the ever-patient editor Gillian Haslam, but also with a new copy editor, Lee Faber, and a wonderful book designer, Christine Wood. Thank you for your priceless help in making *The Romantic Prairie Cookbook* beautiful.

But, let's not forget the delicious contributions of the other "accomplices" who so generously shared their recipes, kitchens, gardens, time, hospitality, kindness, and enthusiasm....and who made me gain 8 pounds! Thank you Sarah and Darius Anderson, Helen Barrett, Susie and Ed Beall, Lynn Brewer, Julie Butterfield, Dee Byrnes, Maria Carr, Rebecca Ersfeld, Doreen Frost, Barbara Jacksier, Donna Jenkins, Debra Hall, Sara Higgins, Judi Gallagher, Debra and Don Germain, Nicole Germain-Perez, Elizabeth and Giampiero Kirkpatrick, Anne Lake, Tracey Leber, Anne Marie, Doug McFarland, Lizzie McGraw, Manhattan Marek, Elizabeth Mears, Joe O'Grady, Robin O'Grady, Lulu Tapp, Angela Reed, Jennifer Rizzo, Jon Paul Saunier, Erin and Jason Shepherd, Caroline Verschoor, Anne Vitiello, Joy and Don Waltmire, Eric Williams, and Beth Zaskey. This book is yours, too.

Lastly, to my "partner in mayhem," Sunday Hendrickson: your exquisite touch never fails to inspire me and your friendship always comforts me. Thank you.

With much love and gratitude to each and everyone.

xoxo *Fifi*
http://fabulousfifi.typepad.com